What's Missing

What's Missing

Best Practices for Teaching Students with Disabilities

Carolyn Lindstrom and Bonita M. Drolet

ROWMAN & LITTLEFIELD
Lanham • Boulder • New York • London

Published by Rowman & Littlefield
A wholly owned subsidiary of The Rowman & Littlefield Publishing Group, Inc.
4501 Forbes Boulevard, Suite 200, Lanham, Maryland 20706
www.rowman.com

Unit A, Whitacre Mews, 26-34 Stannary Street, London SE11 4AB

British Library Cataloguing in Publication Information Available

Library of Congress Cataloging-in-Publication Data Available

ISBN: 978-1-4758-3409-3 (cloth : alk. paper)
ISBN: 978-1-4758-3410-9 (pbk. : alk. paper)
ISBN: 978-1-4758-3411-6 (electronic)

∞™ The paper used in this publication meets the minimum requirements of American National Standard for Information Sciences—Permanence of Paper for Printed Library Materials, ANSI/NISO Z39.48-1992.

Printed in the United States of America

This book is dedicated to our husbands, Andy Bradvica and Tom Harvey, and our families who encourage our research and writing every day. We are so thankful for your loving support. Additionally, we dedicate this book to the students and educators who will be able to grow and prosper when the ideas presented are implemented.

Contents

Contents

Introduction

Everybody is a genius, but if you judge a fish by its ability to climb a ladder, it will go its whole life believing it is stupid.

Albert Einstein

You have decided you want to be a teacher. You went to school, took required courses, and observed a variety of classroom settings, teaching styles, and students. You wrote papers and researched how to teach students. You passed state and federal exams. You earned your credential and accepted a position teaching in the right school with the right students. Now, you're ready to teach your own class. You have great bulletin boards and desks are arranged and lesson plans are written.

You receive the class roster and get excited. But as you look closer at the class list, you realize some of your students have Individual Education Plans (IEPs) and 504s. The office informs you that you have files for students with medical issues and learning disabilities. There are recommendations from previous teachers about where a particular student should or should not sit. You've been given information about how a student needs certain modifications for reading, writing, and/or listening.

There is even paperwork showing that another teacher began monitoring a student, implementing intervention strategies, but nothing further was done. You are now officially overwhelmed. Where do you begin? This was not what you signed up for. This was not your plan.

Or . . . you are the new special education teacher on site. You have a caseload to manage, your own class full of students, all with a variety of learning issues. The principal expects you to "mainstream" your students to the general education classrooms, but the other teachers are reluctant to work with you. It is frustrating.

Or . . . your school has moved to a full inclusion model, and you are paired with another teacher to co-teach a class. Regardless if you are the education specialist or general curriculum teacher, suddenly co-teaching, implementing strategies, and sharing your planning can be a daunting task.

Well, this book is for you! It will help you navigate the key issues to providing a more inclusive program. This book is based on solid research and will lessen your fears of how to teach students with a variety of learning issues.

The research states there are 10 key factors that all educators should know when providing a successful inclusive program. These factors are:

1. School Culture

2. Least Restrictive Environment

3. Universal Design for Learning

4. Differentiate Instruction

5. Formative Assessment

6. Cooperative Learning

7. Assistive Technology

8. Professional Learning Communities

9. Co-teaching

10. Leadership Support

The research has also proven when educators communicate with a common language, they are better able to work together to meet the needs of each student who enters the classroom. This book will provide that common language for all educators to understand.

Teachers from general education and special education will be able to come together and collaborate, knowing what the other teacher expects and knowing how to achieve it. You will feel confident that "you've got this" when it comes to teaching all students, regardless of disability or identification. It does not matter what the needs of the students are in your classroom; you will have the skills and knowledge to address any issue that is important when teaching in schools today.

HOW DID WE GET HERE?

When the Individual with Disabilities Education Act (IDEA) of 1990 was first passed, it established new guidelines and standards for teaching students with disabilities. Upon its continued reauthorization, Congress determined that an educational system was now in place that could effectively address the needs of students with disabilities within the general education setting, therefore maintaining "high academic standards and clear performance goals for children with disabilities, consistent with standards and expectations for all students in the educational system" (Gordon, 2013, p. 62).

The expectation was that these standards and goals were to be provided in the least restrictive environment, allowing students with disabilities the same access to curriculum as students without disabilities. Therefore, placement for students with disabilities would be first in general education, with as many supports and services as possible, before more restrictive placements could be considered. IDEA states:

Sec. 300.114 LRE requirements.

(a) General.
  (1) Except as provided in Sec. 300.324(d)(2) (regarding children with disabilities in adult prisons), the State must have in effect policies and procedures to ensure that public agencies in the State meet the LRE requirements of this section and Sec. 300.115 through 300.120.
  (2) Each public agency must ensure that—
    (i) To the maximum extent appropriate, children with disabilities, including children in public or private institutions or other care facilities, are educated with children who are nondisabled; and
    (ii) Special classes, separate schooling, or other removal of children with disabilities from the regular educational environment occurs only if the nature or severity of the disability is such that education in regular classes with the use of supplementary aids and services cannot be achieved satisfactorily. (Education, 2016)

This changed the way schools and school districts viewed educating students with disabilities. No longer were these students to be left in the back of the school and forgotten. Students with disabilities were now expected to be a part of the general education classroom or at a minimum, allowed access to the same educational programs provided to the non disabled students. However, this also meant that with more students with disabilities being placed in general education classrooms, teachers were expected to provide educational services to *all* students.

With the support of special education teachers, the inclusion of students with disabilities in the general education classroom requires teamwork, collaboration, and planning. By working together, students can benefit from the practices that include *all* students.

WHO ARE YOUR STUDENTS?

Understanding the range of disabilities being taught in general education classrooms will help all teachers be aware of the educational needs of the students. IDEA has defined 13 categories of disabilities; all, at some level, are appropriate for general education placement. The higher prevalence disabilities are more likely to find their way into the general education classroom, and a teacher with a general, not special, education credential will be teaching the class.

All teachers need to be prepared to provide a variety of ways to address the needs of these students through lesson design and accessibility. According to the Institute of Education Sciences and National Center for Education Statistics, figure 0.1 illustrates the percentage of disabilities identified in the United States as of 2014.

The most common disabilities identified are in the specific learning disability (SLD) category. Many students within a general education classroom are identified in this category based on their difficulty in reading, writing, listening, speaking, spelling, and calculating math. Some disorders identified under SLD are dyslexia, dysgraphia, auditory processing disorder, dyscalculia, language processing disorder, visual perceptual/visual motor deficit, and nonverbal learning disabilities. Approximately 36% of students are identified with SLDs while attending school (Learning Disabilities Association of America, 2016).

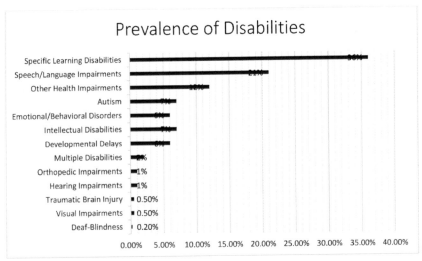

Figure 0.1 Prevalence of Disabilities

Many students, especially younger students, are identified as having communication disorders categorized under speech impairment, which includes speech and language disorders. According to the Center for Disease Control and Prevention (CDC), approximately 8% of students receive services for communication disorders each year, and approximately 21% of students receive services for speech and language (*Children and Youth with Disabilities*, 2015).

Many students with communication or speech/language disorders will need communication accommodations within the classroom setting. Teachers need to be aware of the specific needs of these students. The range of needs can extend from extra time to complete assignments to full communication devices. Teachers must be able to accommodate students to allow full access to the curriculum regardless of their communication ability.

One category that affects the health of students is other health impairments, or OHI. Although OHI does identify many chronic health conditions, such as heart conditions, asthma, and epilepsy, the most common diagnosis for students within a general education setting will be attention deficit hyperactivity disorder (ADHD) (*Children and Youth with Disabilities*, 2015). Depending on the severity of the condition, students with ADHD will typically need a variety of accommodations and modifications to address their behavior, rather than their academic ability. Teachers need to be prepared to provide a variety of behavioral modifications to allow for the specific needs of ADHD students.

Autism is a disability that is affecting more and more students each year. According to the CDC, in 2014 it was reported that the prevalence of Autism had increased by 119.4% from 2000. This is roughly 1 in 150 children diagnosed with a form of autism in 2000 up to 1 in 68 diagnosed by 2010 (Center for Disease Control and Prevention, 2015a). Students with autism can be very high functioning, but need alternative ways to address the curriculum to meet their academic and emotional needs. Awareness and planning must be taken into consideration when providing instruction to these students.

Emotional/behavioral disturbance is a condition identified in students who have long-term emotional issues that adversely affect their ability to learn. Students identified with this disability typically have average intelligence, but their emotional behavior prevents them from learning at the typical rates of their peers. Many are placed in more restrictive classroom settings to meet their specific academic, emotional, and behavioral needs. However, some students are placed in a general education setting. Being aware of their emotional needs will allow for greater success for the student when accessing the general education curriculum.

Students with intellectual disabilities have mental abilities that are typically below those found in students in a general education setting. It could take a longer period of time to assess the needs of students in this category. They must be taught in much different ways. These students are less likely to be placed in a general education classroom, as the services needed are much more intense. They still need access to general education curriculum, but will require modifications and accommodations that allow full access to content. Students with intellectual disabilities typically need functional skill curriculum as well to address cognitive needs.

Students identified with multiple disabilities have more than one disability. Typically these disabilities are at more severe levels, and students may have limited placement in a general education setting. Access to curriculum may have to be provided in a more restrictive environment to allow for services to assist the student in the learning process.

Students identified with orthopedic impairments have conditions that affect their physical abilities and may or may not have accompanying intellectual or learning issues. Students with cerebral palsy, amputations or missing limbs, or other physically limiting conditions will need physical accommodations to allow them full access to the classroom setting, but may or may not need academic accommodations. Teachers need to be prepared to provide alternative ways to assess the physical environment for students identified in this category.

Another disability that will also be found in a general education classroom is students with visual or hearing impairments. These students may or may not have accompanying learning issues. Hearing and visual impairments are sometimes hidden by other disability factors. These students will need to be provided with assistive technologies that allow access to the curriculum. Teachers need to become familiar with a variety of devices so these students can be accommodated in the general education setting.

Students identified with traumatic brain injury (TBI) acquired the injury after birth, and in some cases at an older age. Students diagnosed with TBI need specific teaching techniques to allow for access to the curriculum as their injury could affect only certain parts of the brain, when the student does not necessarily display any outward signs of the trauma. Specific areas of learning could be affected, such as memory or thinking skills. Specific teaching techniques will need to be employed to allow the student to obtain the information in a meaningful way.

According to National Institute of Health (2015), approximately 3 out of every 1,000 children are born with some significant hearing loss in one or both ears. Students who are identified with deaf/blindness or deafness may or may not have accompanying learning issues, but they will need very specific accommodations within the classroom to allow accessibility to the curriculum. Accommodations will be in the form of technology and speaking devices. Teachers will need to be prepared for what this looks like within the classroom setting.

This section began with the question, "Who are your students?" The answer is a multiple-choice one. And, actually, it does not matter. You will have a wide range of students in your classroom, all with varying needs and all requiring access to the curriculum. What you as the teacher need to know is how to address these needs so all students will be successful.

The inclusionary and instructional practices in this book will begin your journey to achieving success for all students. This book does not address specific teaching strategies for students with specific disabilities. It will explain, and demonstrate, how to provide access and include all students in the general education setting. However, for some students, full inclusion is not appropriate. IDEA recognizes that even with support, full access may not work for every student. That does not mean we shouldn't try.

When we include students with disabilities into even some general education instruction, be it art, computers, music, reading, or math, it gives all students the understanding that they can learn and they matter, regardless if it is full inclusion or integrating them into some small part of the curriculum of the day. Yes, it will take time and effort, but eventually, you will see that learning is taking place and that all students can succeed, regardless of their abilities. It is because you took the time to understand them as a person.

BIBLIOGRAPHY

American Academy of Special Education Professionals. (2016, February). *Course #5—Special Education Eligibility.* Retrieved from http://aasep.org/members/professional-development/board-certification-in-special-education-program/certificate-of-advanced-professional-development/special-education-eligibility/index.html

Center for Disease Control and Prevention. (2015a, August 12). *Autism spectrum disorder.* Retrieved from www.cdc.gov

Center for Disease Control and Prevention. (2015b, August 13). *Hearing loss in children.* Retrieved from www.cdc.gov

Education, U.D. (2016). *Building the legacy: IDEA 2004.* Retrieved from http://idea.ed.gov/

Gordon, T.H. (2013). *Individuals with Disabilities Education Act: Handbook for special education teachers and parents* (2nd ed.). Charleston: Createspace.

Learning Disabilities Association of America. (2016). *Types of learning disabilities.* Retrieved from ldaamerica.org

National Institute of Health. (2015, April 20). *National Institute on Deafness and Other Communication Disorders.* Retrieved from www.nidcd.nih.gov

U.S. Department of Education, Institute of Education Sciences, National Center for Education Statistics. (2015, May). *Children and youth with disabilities.* Retrieved from nces.ed.gov

History of Special Education

Every child deserves a champion—an adult who will never give up on them, who understands the power of connection and insists that they become the best that they can possibly be.

Rita F. Peterson

HISTORY

Before we can discuss where we need to be with including all students, it is important to understand how we got here. Inclusion is not a new idea, or a concept made just to add to a teacher's workload; it is a legal requirement that has evolved over the past century to ensure that *all* students, regardless of their physical or mental ability, receive a free and appropriate education that they deserve.

To begin, it must be understood that the U.S. Constitution does not specifically make reference to the public school system. The only reference made to education is, "Responsibility for education therefore lies with the states, which have the authority to determine the scope and organization of their educational systems" (National Constitution Center, 2014). Because of this ambiguity of how the federal government affects public education, there were multiple court cases that addressed educational needs for students during the early part of the twentieth century. Yet, it was not until 1954, when *Brown v. Board of Education* ruled segregation illegal, that education advocates felt hopeful. However, although this landmark decision was groundbreaking for segregation of students with color, it did nothing for students with special needs or disabilities.

The first challenge to "separate but equal," which was the cornerstone for *Brown v. Board of Education*, came in 1965. The Elementary and Secondary

Education Act (ESEA) became the first law that gave federal monies directly to public schools. ESEA established funding limits and legal requirements for institutions and programs that received federal assistance, such as state and local education agencies and universities through programs, otherwise known as Title I.

When ESEA passed in 1965, it provided money to schools for specific populations, yet students with disabilities were not considered as one of these populations. However, within a year of the passage an amendment to ESEA was added that mandated equal educational services to include students with disabilities and, therefore, became the first real legislation that identified students with disabilities a group of students requiring educational services.

Legal Timeline—Separate but Equal

- 1965—Elementary and Secondary Education Act (ESEA)
- 1966—Amendment to include students with disabilities
- 1971—*Pennsylvania Association for Retarded Children v. Commonwealth of Pennsylvania*
- 1972—*Mills v. Board of Education*
- 1973—Section 504 of Rehabilitation Act
- 1975—Education for All Handicapped Children Act (PL 94-142)
- 1990—Individuals with Disabilities Education Act (IDEA)
- 1997—First Reauthorization of IDEA
- 2002—No- Child Left Behind (NCLB)
- 2004—Second Reauthorization of IDEA
- 2007—Individuals with Disabilities Education Improvement Act
- 2009—Common Core State Standards Initiative
- 2015—Every Student Succeeds Act

INCLUSION

A few years later, in 1971 and 1972, two significant court cases that changed drastically how schools responded to students with disabilities emerged. In 1971, *Pennsylvania Association for Retarded Children (PARC) v. Commonwealth of Pennsylvania* overruled a state statute that stipulated a school *could* deny educational services to a child who had been deemed untrainable or uneducable by a school psychologist, or had not reached the mental age of 5 before enrolling in 1st grade and therefore would not benefit from public education. PARC was the first court case that established language identifying a student's right to an individualized education and placement in the least restrictive environment.

Continuing with landmark court cases, in 1972, *Mills v. Board of Education* ruled that schools *could not* deny educational services to students with disabilities because of inadequate funding. Basically stating, schools could not deny students with disabilities an education because of lack of money.

The following year, legislation continued to be created for students with disabilities, and in 1973 Congress passed Section 504 of the Rehabilitation Act. This guaranteed a person, with a disability, could not be excluded or denied access to programs or activities that received federal financial assistance, either public or private. In other words, schools could no longer deny a student's right to education and was now required to offer accommodations for the student when necessary.

Continuing the trend of recognizing the educational needs of students with disabilities, in 1975 President Ford signed one of the most important and game-changing forms of legislation, that is still referred to today: the Education for All Handicapped Children Act otherwise referred to as PL 94-142. This law required a free and appropriate public education (FAPE) to all students with disabilities and outlined the requirement of the IEP.

PL 94-142 continued as the main source of legislation addressing the needs of students with disabilities until 1990 when Congress passed the IDEA. This amended the PL 94-142 and continued to guarantee students with disabilities FAPE and an IEP.

Unlike PL 94-142, IDEA specifically established specific guidelines and principles, detailing how special education and other related services were to be provided to students with disabilities. This form of legislation was the catalyst the inclusionary/accessibility movement needed to guarantee access for students with disabilities.

When President George W. Bush signed No Child Left Behind (NCLB) in 2002, the bill not only amended the Elementary and Secondary Education Act (ESEA) but also expanded the role of the federal government in public education. Up to this point, the federal government directed the financial aspects of public education and stayed away from curriculum issues, leaving that to the state and local organizations. However, NCLB changed the funding of education by placing expectations for student achievement as a requirement for schools to receive resources.

NCLB was praised, at the time, by both political parties and by student advocate groups for raising the expectations for all students, including students with disabilities, and for the first time, students with disabilities were to be assessed using state accountability standards and held accountable for their achievement.

NCLB stated, "Academic standards must apply to all public schools and public school students in the state including public school and public school students served with Title I funds and must include the same knowledge, skills and levels of achievement expected of all students" (United Stated Department of Education, n.d.b).

Therefore, with this level of accountability required for all students, this became a major step toward gaining access to general education curriculum for students with disabilities. It became a major boost in the recognition of special education in the United States. However, this accountability meant that students with disabilities were now expected to be proficient in state standards. Only through fair and equitable access to the curriculum could these students achieve and then be held accountable. So the inclusion of all students became the mantra of many leaders in education.

At the same time that NCLB was really taking root as the assessment/ evaluation requirement in public education, in 2009, a group of governors and commissioners from across the United States formed the Common Core State Standards Initiative (CCSSI). The purpose of this initiative was to set the same standards across all states for students to achieve and be able to compete in a global society as well as be college- and career-ready. Therefore, a common curriculum, along with required assessments, was being implemented in all public schools. States that had adopted the CCSSI were now required to develop plans for implementation and assessment of students, including students with disabilities.

In December 2015, President Barack Obama signed a new education bill that lessened the federal government's role in public schools: the Every Student Succeeds Act (ESSA). This new law still requires annual assessment of subgroups, including students with disabilities; however it does not allow assessments based on modified academic standards. Therefore only students with severe disabilities can be assessed with an alternative assessment. This means that students with learning disabilities must have full access to general education content, as they will be assessed in the same manner as their non-disabled peers. With this new legislation it becomes imperative that all students be given access to general education curriculum in any way possible.

So where are we today? And more importantly, what should we be doing for students with disabilities? We now know through a plethora of research that in order for students to be successful and included in general education, there are specific instructional strategies and inclusionary practices that must be implemented that can address the educational needs of students, especially students with disabilities. In a study conducted in 2015 of elementary schools in four Southern California counties, it was revealed there were key instructional and inclusionary practices that could be contributed to the success of students with disabilities and allow them greater access to general education curriculum (Lindstrom, 2015).

In this book, these practices will be identified, explained, and highlighted with actual scenarios to demonstrate how to implement each practice given any population of students, age level, and/or ability. This book will help all teachers, new and experienced, understand that all students can learn, and that it is their responsibility to find those ways that will work so all students can achieve to the best of their abilities in the most inclusive environment available.

BIBLIOGRAPHY

Allbritten, D., Mainzer, R., & Ziegler, D. (Winter 2004). NCLB: Failed schools—or failed law? Will students with disabilities be scapegoats for school failures? *Educational Horizon, 82*(2), 153–160.

Apling, R., & Jones, Nancy Lee. (2002, January 11). The Individuals with Disabilities Education Act (*IDEA*): Overview of major provisions. *CRS Report for Congress,* 1–6.

Congress, 1. (2001). *Public law 107–10 "No Child Left Behind"* (p. 1439). Washington, DC: United States Congress.

Congress, 1. (2002). "No Child Left Behind Act of 2001." *Public Law 107, 10,* 1–670.

Crawford, J. (2011, February). *Reauthorization of the Elementary and Secondary Education Act (ESEA) . . . and the policy issues at stake.* Retrieved from http://www.diversitylearningk12.com

Department of Education. (2003a). Standards and assessment, non-regulatory guidelines. *No Child Left Behind.* Retrieved from http://www2.ed.gov/programs/titlei parta/legislation.html.

Driscoll, A., & Nagel, N. G. (2010, July 20). *Individuals with Disabilities Education Act (IDEA).* Retrieved from http://www.education.com

Eckes, S., & Swando, J. (2009). Special education subgroups under NCLB: Issues to consider. *Teachers College Record, 111*(11), pp. 2479–2504.

Edsource. (2014). *2012–2013 Title 1 program improvement status statewide summary of schools.* Retrieved from http://www.edsource.org

Esteves, K. J., & Rao, S. (2008, November/December). *The evolution of special education: Retracing legal milestones in American history.* Retrieved from http://naesp.org/resources/1/Principal/2008/N-Oweb2.pdf

Frostburg State University Psychology Students. (2016, January). *IDEA/IDEIA: Individuals with Disabilities Education Act.* Retrieved from http://faculty.frostburg.edu/mbradley/disabilities/IDEA.html#P4

Goertz, M. E. (2005). Implementing the No Child Left Behind Act: Challenges for the states. *Peabody Journal of Education, 80*(2), 73–89.

Heise, M. M. (1994). Goals 2000: Educate America Act: The federalization and legalization of educational policy. *Fordham Law Review, 63*(2), pp. 345–382.

Lindstrom, C. (2015).

Martin, E. W., Martin, R., & Terman, D. L. (1996, Spring). The legislative and litigation history of special education. *The Future of Children: SPECIAL EDUCATION FOR STUDENTS WITH DISABILITIES, 6*(1), 25–39.

National Constitution Center. (2014). The Constitution of the United States. (N. C. Center, Compiler) Philadelphia, Pennsylvania, United States: Library of Congress. Retrieved from www.constitutioncenter.org

Obiakor, F. E., Harris, M., Mutua, K., Rotatori, A., & Algozzine, B. (2012). Making inclusion work in general education classrooms. *Education and Treatment of Children, 35*(3), pp. 477–490.

Osborne, A. G., Jr., & Russo, C. J. (2006). *Special education and the law, A guide for practitioners.* Thousand Oaks, CA: Corwin Press.

Paths to Improving Education: Why Inclusion? (2015, Winter). *The Special Edge, 29*(1), 3–5.

Special Education History—What Is Special Education? (2012). Retrieved from http://www.specialeducationbehaviormodification.com/articles/special_education_history.html

State of Washington Office of Superintendent of Public Education. (n.d.). *Elementary and Secondary Education Act (ESEA).* Retrieved from http://https://www.k12.wa.us/esea/NCLB.aspx

United States Department of Education. (n.d.a). *Building the legacy: IDEA 2004.* Retrieved from http://idea.ed.gov/

United Stated Department of Education. (n.d.b). *No Child Left Behind—Elementary and Secondary Education Act.* Retrieved from http://www2.ed.gov/nclb/landing.jhtml

United States Department of Education. (2015, October 5). *Programs—Improving basic programs operated by local educational agencies (Title I, Part A).* Retrieved from http://www2.ed.gov/programs/titleiparta/index.html

Warren, E. (1976). *The annals of America: Brown et al v. Board of Education of Topeka et al.* (p. 257). Chicago: Encyclopedia Britannica.

Wenkart, R. D. (2002). The No Child Left Behind Act. *Schools Legal Service, Orange County Department of Education.*

Winzer, M. A. (2006). Confronting difference: An excursion through the history of special education. *The SAGE Handbook of Special Education,* 21–33.

Wright, P. (2010, November 19). *The history of special education law.* Retrieved from http://www.wrightslaw.com/law/art/history.spec.ed.law.htm

WrightsLaw. (2014). *Board of Education of Hendrick Hudson Central School District, Westchester County, et al v. Amy Rowley et al.* Retrieved from http://www.wrightslaw.com

Yell, M. L., Rogers, D., & Rogers, Elisabeth Lodge. (1998, July/August). The legal history of special education, what a long strange trip it's been! *Remedial and Special Education, 19*(4), 219–228.

Chapter 1

What Is School Culture?

The role of a creative leader is not to have all the ideas; it's to create a culture where everyone can have ideas and feel that they're valued.

Sir Ken Robinson

School culture is that elusive, but dynamic presence of beliefs, perceptions, relationships, attitudes, and written and unwritten rules or norms that form and impact every aspect of how a school functions and its members behave. School culture also deals with how a school enhances and accepts diversity. Diversity addresses race, ethnicity, gender, and disability. This examination is particularly important for students with disabilities as they may receive more targeted discrimination and negative feedback.

A Resource and Promising Practices Guide for School Administrators & Faculty, published by the University of the State of New York and the New York State Education Department, states, "Establishing and sustaining a school environment free of harassment, bullying, and discrimination should involve an examination of a school's climate and culture. School climate and culture have a profound impact on student achievement, behavior, and reflects the school community's culture" (http://www.p12.nysed.gov/dignity act/rgsection1.html).

The school community's culture determines whether students feel safe, included, and supported in their academic, social, and emotional endeavors. Students with disabilities, as well as all students, will achieve if the following needs are met through the culture of the school. Schools must look at the social environment, physical environment, and emotional environment expectations and support to fully understand and implement a positive

1

school culture. Each of these areas consists of multiple items that must be addressed.

Social Environment

- Interpersonal relations among students and staff
- Respect for diversity
- Emotional well-being and sense of safety
- Student engagement
- School and family collaboration
- Community partnerships

Physical Environment

- Building conditions
- Physical safety
- School-wide protocols
- Classroom management

Emotional Environment

- Physical and mental well-being
- Prevention and intervention services
- Behavioral accountability

Social environment is what provides students with a feeling of well-being. Does the student have friends? Do staff and students recognize differences as a positive force on campus, so there is a rich, diverse culture appreciation? Are students engaged throughout the day? Are they called on equally? Do they feel like their input is valued in class? Is there a sense that collaboration, both for students and for staff, is a vital part of the learning process? Is there a sense of community that is prevalent both on campus and in the wider public arena? If the answer to all of these questions is *yes*, then a student's social environment is strong and supportive.

The physical environment concerns relate to the actual conditions of the buildings and classrooms. Is there a fresh coat of paint applied when needed? Is the building a place you would like to spend 8 hours a day? Is the color scheme and classroom décor conducive to real learning? In order to have a safe physical environment, students must be able to answer *yes* to these questions.

Now that the student is through the front door and sitting in a classroom, the next logical requirement is for personal safety. Is it possible for the student to walk to school and not feel threatened? What about once the entrance to the school has occurred? A student who doesn't feel a safe culture is all encompassing will have difficulty learning. What steps is the school making to ensure everyone's safety? Are there protocols, norms, and disciplinary actions in place that are consistently addressed, made public, and followed?

And lastly, with the protocols, norms, and discipline in place, how do teachers manage their classrooms? Are they orderly and conducive to learning? Do students feel safe to speak out? The physical environment is critical to learning. Going over the list and the questions is not a one-time process, but one that should be engrained in the culture.

Emotional expectations are the final equation in developing a positive culture for learning for all students. What is expected of students? Are the norms for behavior well publicized and well known by students, and are the consequences made apparent to all? Are there a variety of intervention and, more importantly, prevention services available for staff and students to call upon when needed? Are students held accountable for their actions in a dignified way that promotes learning and behavior change? Are slip-ups OK, or does the hammer come down every time? Students want and need clear direction and clear consequences. They may not verbalize the need, but it is there and it is up to the school staff to work collaboratively to enforce common behavioral expectations.

Together, the *social environment*, the *physical environment*, and *emotional expectations* make up this thing we call culture. Culture has many fine aspects that need careful attention.

Dr. David Osher, of American Institutes for Research, and Dr. Chris Boccanfuso, of Child Trends Safe and Supportive Schools Technical Assistance Center and American Institutes for Research, have developed the following matrix to assist schools in their quest for a more positive culture. (See figure 1.1.)

Examining each of these factors, safety, support, challenge, and social capability in detail will allow school personnel to determine current practices, make changes, and monitor the success of the policies as well as the students.

A positive school climate results in better attendance and student success, which translates into higher promotion and graduation rates for students. Achieving a positive school culture is not difficult, but it does take determination and a focused vision for what a school should be for students. A positive school culture does not happen by itself. It takes determination, consistency, advocacy, and knowledge of what drives a positive learning culture.

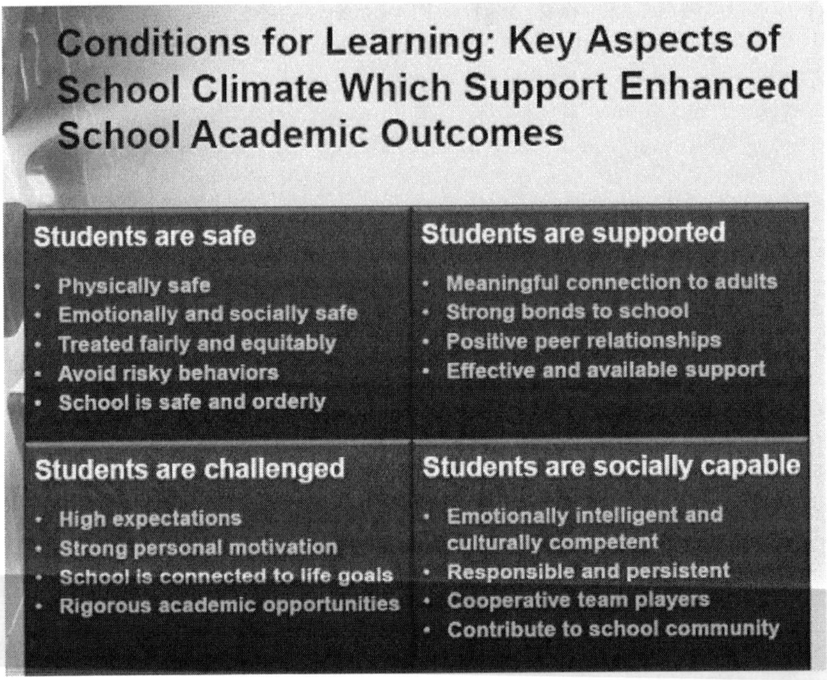

Conditions for Learning: Key Aspects of School Climate Which Support Enhanced School Academic Outcomes

Students are safe

- Physically safe
- Emotionally and socially safe
- Treated fairly and equitably
- Avoid risky behaviors
- School is safe and orderly

Students are supported

- Meaningful connection to adults
- Strong bonds to school
- Positive peer relationships
- Effective and available support

Students are challenged

- High expectations
- Strong personal motivation
- School is connected to life goals
- Rigorous academic opportunities

Students are socially capable

- Emotionally intelligent and culturally competent
- Responsible and persistent
- Cooperative team players
- Contribute to school community

Figure 1.1   Conditions for Learning
Source: American Institutes for Research (AIR), with permission.

SCENARIO

Mr. Harvey had just transferred to a new school as the resource teacher. As he approached his new classroom, he noticed that all the teachers were in their rooms. It was pretty quiet, and no one had welcomed him. After sitting in his bare room trying to figure out what to do next, he had an idea.

I need to go introduce myself to staff members and find out how things work around here.

He proceeded to go from one classroom to another and met a nice group of people. Finally, he decided he needed to do more than introduce himself. He entered the last classroom in his wing.

Tom: Hi. I'm Tom Harvey. I'm the new resource teacher.

Maureen: Hello Tom, I'm Maureen Blair and I teach 5th grade.

Tom: (then began to ask questions) Tell me about the neighborhood? Is it a safe place for students?

Maureen: Many of the students walk, because their parents work and there isn't any busing except for our students in the special education program. I worry sometimes because some of the students have to walk through some pretty tough areas.

Tom: What has the school done to make it safer for the students?

Maureen: Well, we try to make it safer. The principal goes around to the community and talks about how student safety to and from school is paramount to their learning. It has seemed to help. At the end of last year there were far fewer incident reports about issues to and from school. I wish we could do the same here at school!

Tom: Wow, what is happening here?

Maureen: It's really difficult for us all to get on the same page. Our previous resource teacher thought the rules were too hard for her kids and tended to ignore the consequences. To be fair, she wasn't the only one. Students began to realize that their behavior really relied on who was on duty and whose class they were assigned to. It's been hard to fight that. The principal means well, but she hasn't stepped in to make changes to our culture.

Tom: Are the norms and consequences posted or written somewhere?

Maureen: Yes, we have a student handbook and staff handbook.

Tom: What resources are available for students having behavior or academic issues?

Maureen: We have a school psychologist who is here one day a week, and she tries to meet with a small group of students having behavior issues, but sometimes emergencies come up or new students enroll that need her immediate evaluation, so it's not really consistent. We just started intervention for our Tier 1 students. There's an afterschool program for students having difficulty with English and language arts.

Tom: Not for math? What about the students in the special education program?

Maureen: No, nothing for math yet. We haven't included the students in the special education program yet because they have such specific IEPs.

Tom: How do you think the academic expectations are handled?

Maureen: Well, some of these kids come from difficult situations at home, so we try not to put too much pressure on them. We try to do what we can. And before you ask, we try hard to meet the IEP goals and even that is sometimes difficult!

Tom: It sounds like there is some work to do to promote a more positive culture. Do you think the principal would be willing to let me help?

I just finished a class on leadership and promoting a positive school culture for student success.

Maureen: I really think she would love the help. She's worked hard with the community to make the way to school safe. I'm sure she would like some support to keep the momentum going. How would you change the culture?

STRATEGIES FOR CHANGING SCHOOL CULTURE

1. Analyze the Situation

Unless you take the time to analyze the culture, you may select the wrong strategy or make a misstep in the sequence of what needs to be accomplished. There are a plethora of survey that can be implemented for analysis:

- Characteristics of Effective Teams Survey, *Building Teams, Building People*, Harvey and Drolet, 2004
- Principal Self Survey, *Building a Bridge to Success: From Program Improvement to Excellence*, pp. 122–126, Drolet and Turner, 2010
- *Building Strong School Cultures*, pp. 68–70, Kruse and Louis
- School Culture Triage Survey and Audit, Wagner and Masden-Copas
- Megan Tschannen Moran's Scale, http://mxtsch.people.wm.edu/research_tools.php
- West Ed's Healthy Kids School Climate Survey, http://www.wested.org/chks/pdf/scs_flyer_04.pdf

Once you have completed your analysis, it is time to determine your barriers to change. This identification process is crucial in order to detect who wants to make a culture change and who likes things the way they are. There are two excellent books that will help you in this endeavor:

- *Checklist for Change*, Harvey, 1995
- *Resistance to Change*, Harvey and Broyles, 2010.

2. Develop Core Tenets/Values

The next step in changing a culture is to bring your staff and parents together, either as a large group with representatives from each group or as two smaller groups. It will be these groups' task to identify the core tenets and values that the school should be known for. Dialogue about what is important, what values the students should have leaving the school, and what the community will relate to about the school. Once the group has had an opportunity to have some discussion, proceed with a Snow Card activity.

- Have each member write on five 3 × 5 cards the values they think are most important for the school.
- After 5 minutes have each member find another. Together they will have 10 cards.
- Have the pairs come to consensus on 6 of the values.
- Now have the pairs find another pair. There will be 4 people and 12 cards.
- Have this foursome come to consensus on 8 values.
- At any time the group members can get new cards to write a value that they hadn't thought of previously.
- Have cards posted on a wall with different topics going across and the same topics under each other.
- Looking at the cards that garnered the most comments, write 6–8 tenet/ value statements that will represent the core beliefs of the school; that is, we care for each and every member of our school community.
- Share with the parent group if none are on the committee. Let as many groups as possible have input into the tenet/core value statements.
- Incorporate them in written and oral communication.
- Revisit them often.

3. Determine the Shared Vision for the Future

The next step is to preferably use the same group that developed the core values, but some leaders choose to have more people involved and will select a new group to write the vision statement. Whichever group is used, begin with the core beliefs as a springboard to develop a shared vision of where the school should be in 5 years. It is important to use metaphors and descriptive language to bring everyone along. Listen to Martin Luther King's "I Have a Dream" speech to get the feel for what a vision statement sounds like. Here's another example of the vision statement from an actual school:

A VISION FOR BR SCHOOL

BR School will be recognized as an invention center, encouraging students, staff and community members to continually explore their environment. It will be a problem-solving center that encourages lifelong learning.

BR will offer a unique program for students and be an integral part of the greater community. Its facilities, resources and philosophy will meet the varied learning needs and interests of its diverse participants during the school day and through afterschool activities. Excited, involved learners of all ages will focus on inventing the future.

BR staff will act to heighten students' enthusiasm to become lifelong Explorers. The active involvement of adults as parallel and collaborative learners seeking solutions will be essential in this process.

BR students will be provided programs that will allow them to continually explore the unknown and experience success in their endeavors. Real life issues will become the catalyst for exploring possible solutions and applying a variety of problem solving methods. Students will experience learning through hands on activities, use of technology, and active research in independent and cooperative settings.

These ideas and resources will empower students of BR to focus on knowledge acquisition and creation of new ideas supported by technology. The home and school will work collaboratively to extend the physical base for learning. A nurturing, encouraging and caring environment will propel our lifelong learners along their education journey as they "Reflect on the Past, Explore the Present, and Invent the Future."

Once the vision is finalized, include it when talking about the future of the school, in written correspondence, and on banners. Select artifacts, a motto, songs, and a mascot that communicate the vision. Everyone will be on the same page, and the school begins to move toward a positive school culture!

4. Develop Norms for Behavior

Now that the core values and vision are in place, it's time to turn to staff norms for behavior. It's important to include the entire staff. Let the staff determine how everyone will behave.

A good way to accomplish this is to divide the entire staff into small groups and have each group chart every norm that exists. Some will be explicit, such as "We will all be on time for duty." Others may be implicit, "Don't sit in Gwen's chair in the lounge." Whether explicit or implicit, they should be written down on the charts. Some norms may have a positive tone, such as "We will use respectful language when speaking to students." Or they may have a negative tone, such as "Everyone is late for meetings." All are written down.

Post the charts around the room. Then give everyone 10 minutes or more, depending on the size of the staff, to mark five norms that are really important to them. They may be explicit already, or they may be an implicit norm that needs to be more explicit. Also, a mark can be placed at a negative norm as the one stated earlier, "Everyone is late for meetings" in order for it to be changed to an explicit positive norm like "We will all be on time for meetings."

Turn the norms with the most marks into positive, explicit norms. Eight to 10 norms are plenty. Some examples of norms:

- Meeting norms
  - Meetings will begin and end on time.
  - Everyone will be on time for meetings.
  - People pay attention to the person speaking.
  - There will be a chairperson at all meetings.
- Responsibility norms
  - Responsibilities will be shared equally.
  - We expect personal best from every individual.
  - Providing assistance to colleagues is everyone's responsibility.
- Standards norms
  - Professional attire will be worn at all times.
  - Positive attitudes will be shown with the public at all times.
  - Agreements among the group will be honored by all.
- Innovation and change norms
  - Change is considered a positive activity.
  - Suggestions for improvement will be encouraged.
  - Risk taking is important and will be supported.

Once the norms are finalized, it is important to hold people accountable for adhering to or violating the norms. In order to do this it is necessary to review the norms on a regular basis. It is recommended to review one norm each staff meeting. Having the staff members "check in" with themselves and their colleagues will strengthen the norms and provide a positive school culture!

5. Promote Shared Leadership

Everyone has a strength when it comes to leadership. It is important to find out each and every one. Discover the strengths of every member of the staff by first asking each person individually what they think their strength is when it comes to leadership. Use those strengths to encourage leadership behavior from everyone.

Share your observation of the strengths you see. For instance, one teacher may have a great way to engage students in the classroom. Ask that teacher if mentoring the student council would be something to try. Another teacher may have a very analytical mind. That teacher might want the opportunity to be in charge of parent surveys.

There are many ways for teachers and other staff members to lead. Don't be afraid to ask. Whether you are the principal, teacher, or other staff member, ask! You might be surprised by the positive response.

6. Analyze the Data

In order to change the culture it is important to analyze all of the student data just as you analyzed the culture data in the first step. There are many types of data to analyze. It is important to disaggregate the data down to a point where you can say, "We need to focus on the students in the Special Education program who are placed in full inclusion and who are struggling in English Language Arts."

- Academic (formative and summative)
  a. English-language learners
  b. Special education
  c. Ethnicity
  d. Socioeconomic
  e. Foster children
- Attendance
- Discipline
- Expulsions
- Student Attendance Review Board (SARB)
- Individual Education Plan (IEP)
- 504 Plans

Use the data in developing goals and outcomes. The data should direct you to distinct goals for achievement and student success. This is an ongoing process in staff meetings, grade-level or department meetings, and professional learning communities (PLCs).

7. Write Clear Goals and Expected Outcomes Derived from the Data

Develop teams of teachers and staff members to work on various goals that arise out of the data. In the preceding example that states, "We need to focus on students in the Special Education program who are placed in full inclusion and who are struggling in English Language Arts" the goal could be that "All students with disabilities placed in full inclusion classrooms will increase their English Language Arts Benchmark score by one rubric score each semester."

Once each group has developed their goals with an expected outcome, present them to the staff for input and needed changes. Determine timelines for each goal and then write simple and doable action plans. Be sure to put in place an accountability system. Who will keep us on track? Who will call attention to a redirect? Focus on the fact these goals with a stated curricular focus are the responsibility of all staff members.

8. Set High Expectations

One of the best ways to change the culture is to set high expectations for everyone. Students want it and staff want it. Sometimes they just don't know it! Whether it is high expectations for dress, behavior, or academics, make them clear to the students and staff members. Accept "no excuses" and be consistent! These expectations can be an outgrowth of the goals and action plans or from the core values. They need to be explicit!

9. Develop a Communication System

Building relationships through communication is an important part of the schooling process and strengthening the school culture. Make sure everyone is on a need-to-know basis—don't leave people out of the loop. Most communication isn't important to everyone until they don't receive it! Then it becomes the most important piece of information. So be sure your system, whether it be paper, email, social media, or newsletters, gets to the right people in a timely fashion.

Schedule collaboration time so staff members can communicate with each other. They can also determine what issues are lurking out there waiting to pounce! Communication is the key to combating rumors, gossip, and myths! Be sure that parents are included often and more often. They are your best resources in communicating your vision, core values, and goals. Use them appropriately. Be sure to set expectations for communication and collaboration with every group on campus.

10. Incorporate a Shared Decision-Making Process

Making good decisions is hard work! Include the whole staff or a leadership team as needed. Include problem finding as well as problem solution. A good resource is *The Practical Decision Maker*, by Thomas Harvey, Bill Bearley, and Sharon Corkrum. It has many decision-making processes for any problem that may arise. You will keep it handy once you implement one of the strategies!

11. Encourage Shared Tasks

One of the best ways to build a team to support the school culture is to figure out "who can lead?" and "who can be involved?" in the accomplishment of tasks. Intuitively, leaders go to the same people over and over, but practically, it is better to spread out the leadership tasks in order to build more leaders. Once that is done it's time to assign groups to complete the tasks. The more people work together as a team to accomplish shared tasks, the stronger they become.

Encourage everyone. It works in classrooms as well. We think we know who can accomplish a task, but do we really? Have we explored other options to let others shine a light on their talent? Use cooperative learning and watch what happens over time. Students will emerge as leaders, and students will begin to work better and better on shared tasks. It's worth a try!

12. Provide for a Safe Environment

Students and staff members need to know they are safe to work at an optimal level. What does the school look like? Does it appear safe in today's world, or are changes to the physical plant a necessity? Are they being given a priority? Giving students a safe environment will free up their minds to learn and reach the goals you have laid out for them. Giving staff members a safe place will encourage them to be their best at all times.

Is there a clear discipline plan in place that focuses on behavior, elimination of bullying, and respect for all learners and staff members? Students of all ages want clear boundaries, whether they act that way or not. It is our job as educators to make sure that those boundaries are in place in a respectful way. Students should be aware of all the consequences of their behavior.

One principal had students call their parents and lay out the entire situation as the principal listened to the students. Most of the students could tell their parents the consequences of their actions without even talking to the principal! The student discipline was consistent, fair, and safe for all the students.

The same discipline plan needs to be activated in all the classrooms simultaneously. Students should know from one year to the next or one class to the next that the rules are the same. They can feel safe in their environment, and therefore, they can learn!

13. Plan Celebrations/Recognitions—Large and Small

Celebrations aren't just for birthdays or milestone events, they are for every day! for success of the school goals, for staff accomplishments, for student achievement and attendance. These events should be honored and celebrated often.

One principal called a monthly assembly for the entire school. At this assembly the principal announced every success. Whether a teacher received a master's degree or a student was acknowledged for a curricular success, cheers went up. One assembly honored the custodian who had become a citizen and some of the staff dressed as American symbols such as the Statue of Liberty and the Bald Eagle.

Celebrations don't always have to be assemblies; they can be notes of encouragement to a staff member who is making progress with a student. They can be recognizing students for learning to read or master complicated math equations. They can be for students who have accomplished an IEP Goal. The list of celebrations for successes can go on and on. The important thing is to have them! In this way you are establishing joyous traditions that build a positive culture that helps all students learn and have confidence in their learning ability.

14. Encourage Storytelling

Storytelling is an important part of building a positive school culture. Why? Every time a new staff member arrives on campus, like Tom in our scenario, they are adrift. They are not sure how to act, what to do, or what to say. The more they hear about the traditions, the celebrations of the past, what is going well, who is a hero, staff members will begin to belong.

They will want to buy into such a vibrant culture that honors the past. They will want to help preserve the present by reinforcing high expectations and outcomes so stories can be told in the future about how great it was then and how great it will continue to be. And don't forget about students! Telling success stories at assemblies or in student newspapers spreads the word about positive behaviors, attitudes, and results!

One principal started every staff meeting with the following question:

"What was a surprise in your classroom that lead to increased student learning?" Teachers were able to share, first in small groups and then to the whole group. Storytelling became a way to change behaviors, attitudes and strategies as teachers listened to one another and mulled over how it might work in their classroom.

The end of the year found these questions being posed by the principal:

"How have you changed this year?"
"What students were involved in your change?"

SUMMARY

The result of implementing these actions will be the building of trust and a positive school culture. They are presented in a loose order of implementation. Obviously, without an analysis, it would be difficult to know where to begin. Values must be articulated and a vision developed in order to know what path your school will be on. Schools may need all 14 steps or fewer. Depending upon need, it is imperative that every step be implemented eventually to change a culture.

As more and more people become engaged in the process of schooling, the environment will begin to change—slowly at first—there will be tremendous resistance to change. Eventually, the staff, parents, and students will understand that the changes that take place are a result of their input, their needs, and their desires. The school will shed its toxic characteristics and put in its place a warm and caring environment that promotes learning. It will be transformed into a positive culture! Tom and all the other teachers and staff will love to be there. Students will excel and be joyful!

BIBLIOGRAPHY

Boccanfuso, D. (2016, June). *School climate.* Retrieved from https://safesupportive-learning.ed.gov.

Broyles, T. and Harvey, T. (2010). *Resistance to change, A guide to harnessing it positive power.* Lanham, MD: Rowman & Littlefield.

New York State Department Education (2016, March). *A resource and promising practices guide for school administrators & Faculty.* Retrieved from http://www.p12.nysed.gov/dignityact/documents/FINALDignityForAllStudentsActGuida nce-May2016.pdf.

Drolet, B. (2010). *Changing toxic school cultures—Policy paper #12.* University of La Verne. La Verne: EPIC.

Harvey, Thomas, Bonita M. Drolet and Douglas P. DeVore. (2014). *Leading for excellence: A twelve step program to student achievement.* Lanham, MD: Rowman & Littlefield.

Oscher, D. (2011). *Making the case for the importance of school climate and its measurement in turnaround schools.* Washington, DC: National Center on Safe and Supportive Learning Environments, American Institutes for Research.

Drolet, B., & Turner, D. (2010). *Building a bridge to success: From program improvement to excellence.* Lanham, MD: Rowman & Littlefield.

Chapter 2

What Is Least Restrictive Environment?

We know that equality of individual ability has never existed and never will, but we do insist that equality of opportunity still must be sought.

Franklin D. Roosevelt

Through the years of Individuals with Disabilities Act (IDEA) we have heard that all students should be placed in the least restrictive environment. What does this mean? IDEA is very specific in its description of how placements should be determined for students with disabilities.

Least Restrictive Environment (LRE) is the requirement in federal law that students with disabilities receive their education, to the maximum extent appropriate, with nondisabled peers and that special education students are not removed from regular classes unless, even with supplemental aids and services, education in regular classes cannot be achieved satisfactorily. [20 United States Code (U.S.C.) Sec. 1412(a)(5)(A); 34 Code of Federal Regulations (C.F.R.) Sec. 300.114.] (Disability Rights California, 2011)

In other words, LRE is the placement of a student in the proper educational environment, being a classroom, school, or outside setting that provides the best opportunity to access the curriculum with the least amount of services and supports.

For most students, this is the general education classroom with a general education teacher. For students with learning disabilities, depending on the severity, a student could be placed in general education with consultation with special education teacher or other service providers, for example, speech or occupational therapist or a paraprofessional working within the classroom to provide additional support to the teacher and the students. In some instances, a student may be assigned a paraprofessional to assist in behavior or emotional management that does not adversely affect his or her ability to access the curriculum.

For students who need more support, there are, in some districts, resource teachers. These are education specialists who work with specific students with IEP either in the classroom or in a separate room. Many times a resource teacher may co-teach with a general education teacher for specific subjects within a school day.

Depending on the needs of the student and the structure of the program at your school site, student support may be done with a "push-in" or "pull-out" model. Students requiring this level of service are taught general education curriculum; however some accommodations, or modifications, may be needed to allow accessibility.

For students with more intense learning issues, the appropriate placement may be in a self-contained day class (SDC). This is a separate class taught by a special education teacher, for students identified with moderate, severe, or profound disabilities. Students with this level of disability are still expected to have access to the general education curriculum, and it will require planning and cooperation to provide the proper level of access. Scaffolding the curriculum to meet the level of the student's ability will have to take place.

Students within this environment benefit from being included in as many general education functions as possible. Students with this level of disability may benefit from being fully included within the general education classroom; however it will require teamwork between both special and general education teachers to make for a successful program.

There are two additional placements typically not found within the school or district boundaries. Residential placement is a very restrictive placement assigned to students whose emotional or behavioral actions require more supervision and/or support than can be provided within a public school setting. Trained professionals, along with trained special education teachers, work with the students in a setting away from public school. The students are still given access to the general education curriculum. Typically, these students do not have cognitive deficiencies that affect their learning, but other factors prevent them from accessing services in a public school setting.

When students are so severely sick or have such profound learning or physical issues, they cannot attend public school and they are placed in a home or hospital setting. These students are still required to have access to general education curriculum, and either the district will provide a teacher to teach them at home or the hospital will provide a teacher for their school requirement. Some students at this level may have issues that access to general education curriculum is limited. Teachers need to assess the student's abilities to learn the material and adjust accordingly.

Schools must always consider general education classrooms as the first placement for all students. Only after it is determined that a student cannot sufficiently access the general education curriculum, even when supported with aides and/or services, should alternative placements be considered in other settings. This is referred to as continuum of alternative placement (CAP). Educators should always consider the least restrictive environment as the first placement for students with disabilities, then more restrictive placements when students need more services to access the general education curriculum.

FULL INCLUSION IS NOT FOR EVERY STUDENT

It is important to understand that not all students can, nor should be, fully included. Inclusion practices will vary widely from district, county, and state. Some schools/districts provide different placements in accordance with legal requirements, but teachers can still implement many of the instructional strategies to allow for greater access to general education curriculum.

When discussing least restrictive environment, it must be understood that it not only is about location, but it is also about access. It is about what is taught and how it is presented. Least restrictive environment is about providing access to the general education curriculum for students with disabilities.

There are many ways of providing access that can be beneficial to all students. When considering placement, one must consider what is best for the student, academically, socially, and emotionally. The level of access for students with disabilities ranges from full inclusion in a general education classroom to complete separation in a different school setting. Although full inclusion is the expectation of successful schools, it may not be appropriate for every student.

The CAP is a chart of the alternative placements available for students with disabilities within public education that identifies the different levels of placement from least restrictive to most restrictive. (See figure 2.1.)

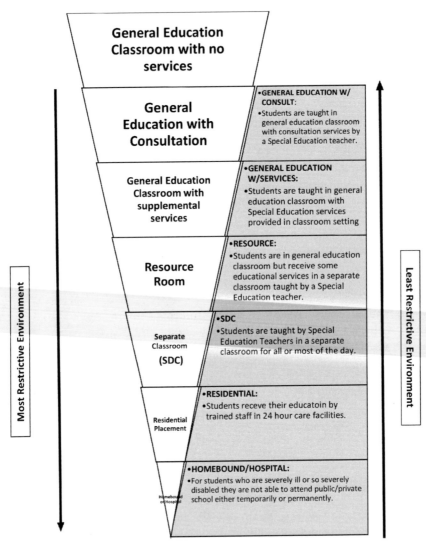

General Education Classroom with no services

General Education with Consultation

•GENERAL EDUCATION W/ CONSULT:
•Students are taught in general education classroom with consultation services by a Special Education teacher.

General Education Classroom with supplemental services

•GENERAL EDUCATION W/SERVICES:
•Students are taught in general education classroom with Special Education services provided in classroom setting

Resource Room

•RESOURCE:
•Students are in general education classroom but receive some educational services in a separate classroom taught by a Special Education teacher.

Separate Classroom (SDC)

•SDC
•Students are taught by Special Education Teachers in a separate classroom for all or most of the day.

Residential Placement

•RESIDENTIAL:
•Students receve their educatoin by trained staff in 24 hour care facilities.

Homebound or Hospital

•HOMEBOUND/HOSPITAL:
•For students who are severely ill or so severely disabled they are not able to attend public/private school either temporarily or permanently.

Most Restrictive Environment

Least Restrictive Environment

Figure 2.1   Least Restrictive Environment

SCENARIO

The school is holding an IEP for Peter, a 7-year-old boy, who has autism spectrum disorder. He has speech and language impairment that limits his ability to communicate; however, his intellectual the ability has been determined to fall within normal range. He has demonstrated ability to understand grade-level math and recognize sight words. He has some behavioral issues due to his limited communication skills.

The team is meeting to determine placement for next year. He is currently in an SDC for students with autism with some mainstreaming for art and Physical Education or P.E. His current special education teacher feels he should be in the general education class more often for academic content. The parents are worried about his behavior. The general education teacher is concerned how he will access the curriculum. The speech and language teacher is working on developing better communication skills, possibly with an augmented communication device (AAC).

In attendance are the principal, Mr. Dean; the speech and language teacher, Ms. Linn; the current special education teacher, Mrs. Cardell; the current general education teacher, Mr. Brooks; the school psychologist, Mr. Michaels; and Peter's mother.

Mrs. Cardell:	Well, I first want to thank everyone for being here this afternoon. I know that we all care about Peter, we want the best for him, and we all want to make sure he is placed in the best class setting as possible.
Mr. Brooks:	I agree. I really have enjoyed having Peter in class for art. He is very creative with his drawings.
Mom:	Yes, he loves to bring home his art and show me what he has done that day. He is so happy on the days he goes to art.
Mr. Brooks:	I know. He gets along with the other students so well, most of the time. He has had his moments, but I know it is when he can't express his thoughts correctly. I know this is very frustrating for him.
Ms. Linn:	Yes, well I have done a communication evaluation on him, and he qualifies for a personal communication device. Beginning next school year, he will have a tablet with a pre-set communication program that will allow him to "talk." I plan to help him during the transition from the picture icons he is currently using to the communication program in class next year. I will increase my minutes for the first semester to accommodate the training he will need.
Mom:	That is fabulous! Will he be able to bring it home?
Ms. Linn:	Yes, and we can set up a plan to have us work with him together.
Mrs. Cardell:	Oh, that would be wonderful. Thank you so much. That will alleviate so many behaviors I am sure.
Mr. Brooks:	That sounds incredible. Will this work in all his classes?

Ms. Linn: Yes, it will be programmed so he can communicate where ever he goes.

Mrs. Cardell: Well, now that we know he will have more support in his communication, we need to move forward and discuss his academics. Mr. Michaels did an academic evaluation and I think he should share the results.

Mr. Michaels: Thank you. Yes, I did do an academic evaluation, and Peter did very well. He was able to achieve at just below grade level in reading and at grade level in math.

Mrs. Cardell: Yes, I agree. I have been able to have Peter work on many grade-level assignments and he does very well. It just has been the lack of communication and then the subsequent behavior that has kept him from fully accessing the curriculum.

Mr. Brooks: Well, I can see that Peter is able to maintain good behavior when engaged in work that he feels comfortable doing. The token system that you suggested Mrs. Cardell really works with well with him.

Mrs. Cardell: Mr. Brooks, I am so glad that is working for Peter. So, based on this information, and given that Peter will have greater support once the new communication tablet arrives, I would like to increase his minutes in general education next year.

Mr. Dean: Well, the intent of the law is that students must be placed in the least restrictive environment. Let me ask, can Peter access the grade-level work with or without support?

Mrs. Cardell: Well, Peter needs some support because he cannot read directions on his own. However, once he understands what needs to be done, he is able to work independently. What would you say Mr. Brooks?

Mr. Brooks: I agree. However, he is only in my class for art and PE. I have not really had him for the academic classes. But, he is a good boy and I can see where he could work independently. Plus, the students know him and many are able to work with him, sometimes better than me.

Mrs. Cardell: I know I have seen that too. These students are wonderful.

Mom: Yes, I have seen them be so helpful to Peter.

Mr. Dean: OK, given that he is capable of accessing the curriculum, with support, I suggest we go ahead and place Peter in the general education class for next year. I will authorize a support person to be with Peter in the class. If necessary, and if we find he needs more support, we can arrange the minutes so he can meet with you, Mrs. Cardell, for a period a few days a week to help him with academics. What does the team think of this arrangement?

Mrs. Cardell: I think this is the best placement option for Peter. He has so many friends and I know with the right support he will do well.

Mr. Brooks: I think that will work. I can share information with his teacher next year and give her ideas on techniques to use with him.

Ms. Linn: Yes, I will make sure to arrange my time with Peter to be available during academic times to support his learning in the class. I will help train his new teacher as well on the tablet.

Mom: I love the placement. Thank you so much for supporting Peter being placed in general education next year.

STRATEGIES FOR LEAST RESTRICTIVE ENVIRONMENT

Ask questions

1. Does the student need support when accessing curriculum? If so, what specific supports?

2. Does the student need assistive technology to access curriculum? If so, what kind?

3. What changes need to be made to the physical environment to allow access to classroom setting?

4. What type of Service Providers will need to be included to allow access to the curriculum?

5. To what degree does the student need accommodations/modifications to access the curriculum?
   - Visit possible classrooms for placements.
   - Maintain open communication with parents/guardians.
   - Develop collaboration time for all providers.
   - Revisit placement, as a team, after 30 days and regularly thereafter to ensure student success.

SUMMARY

Least Restrictive Environment means placement of a student in the school setting that allows them the greatest access to general education curriculum with minimal services to support the student's learning. The placement can range from full inclusion with no support to home/hospital settings.

Depending on the needs of the student and level of ability to access the curriculum will guide the level of placement.

Determining the proper level of placement is the result of decades of legislative reforms and court cases that were intended to recognize that students with disabilities should be held to the highest expectations possible. Providing access to general education curriculum through a wide variety of scientific-based strategies and levels of placements allows all students to achieve. The result is that teachers must be prepared to provide as much access to the curriculum as possible for every student, regardless of disability.

BIBLIOGRAPHY

California Department of Education. (2015). Paths to improving education: Why inclusion? *The SpecialEDge, 29*(1). Retrieved from http://www.calstat.org/publications/article_detail.php?a_id=242&nl_id=134.

Disability Rights California. (2011). Information on least restrictive environment. Retrieved from www.disabilityrightsca.org/pubs/504001Ch07.pdf.

Festus, E. (2012). Making inclusion work in general education classrooms. *Education and Treatment of Children, 35*(3), pp. 477–490.

Hocutt, A. M. (1996). Effectiveness of special education: Is placement a critical factor? *The Future of Children, SPECIAL EDUCATION FOR STUDENTS WITH DISABILITIES, 6*(1), pp. 77–102.

Idol, L. (n.d.). Toward inclusion of special education students in general education: A program evaluation of eight schools. *Remedial and Special Education, 27*(2), 77–94.

Lipscomb, S. (2009, January). Students with disabilities and California's Special Education Program. *Public Policy Institute of California*, San Francisco, CA, pp. 1–37.

Reynolds, B. H. (2008). Are Principals ready to welcome children with disabilities. *Principal*, 16–19, November/December.

Zigmund, N. (2003). Where should students with disabilities receive their special education services? *The Journal of Special Education, 37*(3), 193–199.

Chapter 3

What Is Universal Design for Learning?

If a child can't learn the way we teach, maybe we should teach the way they learn.

Ignacio Estrada

What is universal design for learning (UDL)? The term was developed by David Rose, Anne Meyer, and colleagues at the Center for Applied Special Technology (CAST). It was adapted from the architectural term universal design (UD) that allows full access to all people to buildings, sidewalks, and other publicly accessed properties.

For UDL, there are three basic concepts:

1. Multiple Means of Representation—the *what* of learning
   - present content in different ways
   - adjust content for learning styles, language, levels of intelligence, sensory needs, stages of cognitive development
   - customize content to the student
   - allow for all students to see, hear and touch

2. Multiple Means of Action and Expression—the *how* of learning
   - how will students respond to the information
   - providing different ways for students to express their understanding of the information
   - identify strengths and needs of students
   - continuously assessing for understanding

3. Multiple Means of Engagement—the *why* of learning
   - increase the participation
   - accommodate for cultural backgrounds and interests
   - arrange environment grouping, independent work, and access to technology
   - arrange classroom to allow for student interaction

    CAST—What Is UDL? (http://www.cast.org/research/udl)

The implementation of all three principles brings together a more holistic learning experience for the student. When designing, or developing, a lesson or unit, a teacher must keep in mind the three essential qualities of UDL—representation, expression, and engagement. These core principals contribute to a student's ability to engage in a lesson in a meaningful way.

Multiple Means of Representation addresses students' need of what they are learning. Since every student learns differently, a teacher must provide a variety of ways to present the information so students will be engaged and be motivated in the learning process. Teachers must provide the information using different modalities, such as hearing, seeing, and touching. Students are multisensory learners, and providing the information in a variety of ways allows multiple means of accessing the curriculum.

For example, for students with auditory processing issues, providing text or visual supports for lessons with verbal instructions will allow greater accessibility, just as when a student with visual processing difficulties needs auditory support to interpret the visuals more accurately. These simple accommodations provide access to curriculum in a meaningful way.

Multiple Means of Action and Expression addresses student's need to express what is being learned. Teachers need to allow students to demonstrate understanding of the information in different ways. Some students may be more successful in oral presentation, whereas some will be more effective in visual display of content. Allowing students multiple means to express their understanding will allow them to learn at their rate of comprehension.

Multiple Means of Engagement addresses the student's need to know why he or she is learning. Students have varied backgrounds, and their ability to relate to curricular content varies based on their interest and needs. To have students learn, it is the responsibility of the teacher to find ways to engage every student. A teacher must find the "hook" that will encourage the student to want to learn the information. Whether it is a video, a story, or a more hands-on activity, a variety of approaches will elicit interest. Whatever the means, finding that "right" way allows all students to engage in the lesson and know "why" they are learning.

With the implementation of Common Core State Standards and the need for students with disabilities to have access to the general education curriculum, UDL is a method of instruction that can be used for all students to provide accessibility and understanding of content standards that allow for flexibility in the learning process. UDL maintains the same standards and expectations for every student. It allows access to the curriculum in a way that is best suited for the student.

For students with disabilities to succeed in a Common Core world or under the new ESSA legislation, teachers will need to be familiar with the principles of UDL in order to make the complexity of the standards attainable to all students.

UDL is designed to allow a teacher to teach any type of curriculum, as long as there are multiples means of representation, action and engagement, and expression. This is especially true with Common Core. UDL provides a perfect way to access the curriculum for all students. For teachers, overcoming barriers of access when developing unit lessons is crucial to the implementation of UDL. Addressing barriers can be done by providing alternatives for the same concept but allowing different means of achieving the same goal as shown in figure 3.1.

Multiple Means of Representation	
BARRIER Printed Material—students have visual processing or decoding issues.	*ALTERNATIVE* Students are allowed to research for information using computers or other electronic devices using visual and audio feed.
Multiple Means of Action and Expression	
BARRIER Writing a report—students may have fine motor issues of executive functioning skills and struggle with organization of thoughts or materials.	*ALTERNATIVE* Students demonstrate understanding via multiple means, i.e. poem, play, PowerPoint, recording, diorama.
Multiple Means of Engagement	
BARRIER Students lack engagement due to the limited means of engaging in the lesson.	*ALTERNATIVE* Students have multiples means to engage in the lesson because they can access it via their strengths.

Figure 3.1   Barriers and Alternatives for UDL

SCENARIO

Amy is a student teacher. She is teaching a 4th-grade class. She has 27 students. There are four students with IEPs, three students with 504s, and two students who are mainstreamed from the SDC for social studies. She presented a lesson from the unit on California gold rush. She is meeting with her supervisor for a post-lesson debriefing.

Mrs. Radcliffe: Amy that was a very good lesson you taught. You incorporated some of the UDL principles and teaching strategies that we have discussed over the last few weeks.

Amy: Thanks, Mrs. Radcliffe, I have really been trying to develop ways to address the needs of all the students. I get so worried about how to keep some of the students' attention, as well as make sure that everyone understands the content. For some of them I think it may be too much.

Mrs. Radcliffe: Amy, I agree. Some students in this class are somewhat low academically, and some students are exceptionally high. If you are not careful, you will lose the attention of the higher students, and the low academic students will miss the content. This is what I wanted to discuss today. How do you think you did with addressing the needs of all the students?

Amy: Well, I don't know. With so many levels it felt difficult to meet their needs. So when I was developing the unit, I tried really hard to remember the three guidelines of UDL. I wanted to make sure that every student was able to participate at some level.

Mrs. Radcliffe: Excellent. Let's go over those strategies and see what worked well and what needs to be improved upon for next time.

Amy: Oh that would be great. I am still not sure I completely understand each guideline, nor if I was able to address each principle thoroughly.

Mrs. Radcliffe: Well, let's take each guideline one at a time, and we can discuss how you addressed it throughout the unit.

Amy: Excellent!

Mrs. Radcliffe: Ok, Guideline Number One—Multiple Means of Representation. What did you do for this guideline?

Amy: Well, considering that there were new vocabulary words to be learned for this unit, I wanted to allow the students to acquire the vocabulary in a very meaningful way. So I created a chart that I had penciled in pictures of the key vocabulary words for the unit, and as I told a story about an old man looking for gold, I drew in the pictures with markers so the students would have a visual representation of the words as well as a literary connection.

Mrs. Radcliffe: Amy, I agree that was an excellent way to make multiple connections to the vocabulary. Do you think you could have done anything else to help the students make a connection to the content?

Amy: Well, I could have used more visual or auditory techniques. Maybe watch a short video of a man panning for gold. That would have provided some more contextual ideas. Or, I could have had the students create a vocabulary journal where they draw a picture themselves of the words, allowing more personal connection to the words.

Mrs. Radcliffe: Yes, now you understand even more. Those are good examples of bringing meaning to the content. But what about Shelly? She really seemed uninterested. She has an auditory processing disorder, and I think she was unable to gain the understanding of the vocabulary words you were hoping for. Any thoughts on how you could have made the connection for her?

Amy: I know; she has difficulty following my lessons sometimes. Maybe I could have provided the pictures beforehand so as I drew them she would have had a visual already?

Mrs. Radcliffe: That sounds like a great solution. Good way to differentiate. Also, having her work with another student and discuss the pictures would have benefitted her as well.

Amy: Yes, there are many students who like to work together and would benefit from that. I should not be afraid to let students work together even when I am introducing the lesson. I think it is very beneficial for all students.

Mrs. Radcliffe: All right, let's discuss guideline number two, Multiple Means of Expression. What was one of the ways you allowed the students to share their understanding of the information?

Amy: I thought I did a really good job with this one. After explaining the history of gold rush in California, I wanted them to show the sequence of events so they would understand the cause and effect of the actions of the miners and settlers, so I asked them to make a timeline. I didn't give them any specific directions, other than they were to create a timeline with the dates I provided them. I allowed them to use any type of medium they wanted to share with the rest of the class. I even allowed them to work with a partner or as a trio. I was so pleased when I saw the students share in so many ways. One student drew out his timeline, cutting pictures from a magazine to represent different dates. Three students worked together to make an Animoto™ presentation of the timeline, with music, and two worked on a play they acted out for the class. I was so proud of all the different ways they chose to share their timelines.

Mrs. Radcliffe: Amy, I agree, the different projects the students developed were incredible. Also, it allowed the two students from the SDC class to work with some of the students here and be a part of the assignment. I loved how the one group included Joey in their play, and the fact that Peter, who has some fine motor issues, was able to create his own PowerPoint™ on the computer. Well done Amy.

Amy: Thank you, I am very proud of the results.

Mrs. Radcliffe: Me too. OK let's talk about guideline number three, Means of Engagement. I think you did a great job with the final assignment, but what about throughout the unit? What were some of the ways you kept the students engaged?

Amy: Well, this was a challenge, but I think that the students were engaged with most of the lesson.

Mrs. Radcliffe: Yes, but give me some examples.

Amy: Well, during the reading passages, I did allow some students to take turns reading together. I think this is very effective for students who are slower readers, especially in large groups. I allowed those students with reading challenges to use an audio book to listen to the passages. Also, I allowed those that needed an option of writing out their answer or dictating their answers, to use the tablet. The speech-to-text program was very beneficial to Peter. I think the variety of choices really helped some students stay engaged.

Mrs. Radcliffe: I agree as well. Do you think there were some other ways to help the students stay engaged?

Amy: I don't know, let me think about that. When I was presenting the vocabulary, I could have allowed students to draw their own interpretation of the words. For Shelly, I could have given her the notes beforehand, so when discussing the events she would have had the information in front of her. She had a hard time following along.

Mrs. Radcliffe: Yes, those would have added to the engagement, but overall, I think you did an excellent job with the development of the unit and your ability to create multiple ways for students to be engaged in the lesson.

At times, providing accommodations and/or modifications can seem daunting, given the number of students in the classroom and individual needs; however, with planning, these issues can be addressed before the lesson begins and immediate access can be given to all students.

The following strategies are examples of teaching techniques that will help teachers understand how to address each UDL guideline and principle. (See figure 3.2.)

STRATEGIES FOR UNIVERSAL DESIGN FOR LEARNING

Provide Multiple Means of Representation: WHAT	Examples:
1. Provide options for perception	
1.1 Offer ways of customizing the display of information	Provide options of differing colors to address perception, speed of video, loudness of audio
1.2 Offer alternatives for auditory information	Provide text of speech, ASL for English, visual representations of spoken emotions
1.3 Offer alternatives for visual information	Provide auditory cues for visual transitions, provide description of visual images
2. Provide options for language, mathematical expressions, and symbols	
2.1 Clarify vocabulary and symbols	Pre-teach vocabulary, highlight important text before lesson, embed support of vocabulary into lesson
2.2 Clarify syntax and structure	Align lesson with previous knowledge, highlight transitions between concepts
2.3 Support decoding text, mathematical notation, and symbols	Allow text-to-speech, provide speech device for mathematical numeration
2.4 Promote understanding across languages	Provide key concepts in primary language, allow translation tools
2.5 Illustrate through multiple media	Provide multiple representation of content through variety of forms, i.e. cartoons, music, dance
3. Provide options for comprehension	
3.1 Activate or supply background knowledge	Use advance organizers, link content to previous knowledge, utilize cross-curriculum concepts
3.2 Highlight patterns, critical features, big ideas, and relationships	Highlight key concepts, provide cues and prompts to emphasize important information
3.3 Guide information processing, visualization, and manipulation	Give prompts for sequential learning, allow to use graphic organizers, scaffold learning process of key goals
3.4 Maximize transfer and generalization	Provide a variety of organizational tools, i.e. sticky notes, graphic organizers, mnemonic strategies, provide examples of generalization scenarios

Figure 3.2   Principles of UDL Examples
Source: David H. Rose, 2014, all rights reserved. Reprinted with permission.

Provide Multiple Means for Action and Expression: HOW	Examples:
1. Provide options for physical action	
4.1 Vary the methods for response and navigation	Provide multiple ways to access technology, through touch, speech and eye gaze
4.2 Optimize access to tools and assistive technologies	Utilize ipads, scribe pens, Smartboards
2. Provide options for expression and communication	
5.1 Use multiple media for communication	Provide a variety of communication devices and recordings
5.2 Use multiple tools for construction and composition	Provide different word processing tools such as: label makers
5.3 Build fluencies with graduated levels of support for practice and performance	Provide methods for students to demonstrate understanding through content scaffolding, online websites
3. Provide options for executive functions	
6.1 Guide appropriate goal setting	Allow students to create their learning goals for the lesson based on their level of ability and understanding
6.2 Support planning and strategy development	Provide brainstorming activities, such as mind-maps and student-created study guides
6.3 Facilitate managing information and resources	Graphic organizers or information notebooks
6.4 Enhance capacity for monitoring progress	Graphs and charts
Provide Multiple Means for Engagement: WHY	*Examples:*
1. Provide options for recruiting interest	
7.1 Optimize individual choice and autonomy	Provide multiple topics within the lesson for the student to explore
7.2 Optimize relevance, value, and authenticity	Provide opportunity to make the lesson relevant to current events
7.3 Minimize threats and distractions	Be aware of potential threats and distractions. Provide outlets
2. Provide options for sustaining effort and persistence	
8.1 Heighten salience of goals and objectives	Provide rubrics for students to evaluate their assignments
8.2 Vary demands and resources to optimize challenge	Recognize the different learning levels within the class and provide assignments toward each level
8.3 Foster collaboration and community	Provide cooperative learning opportunities within and outside of classroom
8.4 Increase mastery-oriented feedback	Provide ongoing feedback throughout lesson
3. Provide options for self-regulation	
9.1 Promote expectations and beliefs that optimize motivation	Allow students to set benchmarks for goals to recognize achievement
9.2 Facilitate personal coping skills and strategies	Engage students in activities that highlight coping skills for self and with others
9.3 Develop self-assessment and reflection	Allow students opportunities to reflect on their learning through multiple medias

Figure 3.2 (Continued)

SUMMARY

UDL is the way we should be teaching. It allows *all* students to access the curriculum and allows every student to succeed. As teachers, we must find ways to address the variety of needs of our students, and UDL provides those opportunities. Instead of one approach to learning, teachers can bring multiple approaches and address strengths and areas of need for all students.

BIBLIOGRAPHY

CAST. (2014a, July 14). *UDL & Common Core State Standards.* Retrieved from www.udlcenter.org.

CAST. (2014b, July 31). *What is UDL?* Retrieved from www.udlcenter.org.

Gargiulo, R. M. (2010). *Teaching in today's inclusive classrooms: A universal design for learning approach.* Belmont, CA: Wadsworth, Cengage Learning.

Hitchcock, Chuck, et al. (2002). Providing new access to the general curriculum: Universal design for learning. *Teaching Exceptional Children, 35*(2), 8–17.

The IRIS Center. (2009). *Universal design for learning:Creating a learning environment that challenges and engages all students.* Retrieved from http://iris.peabody. vanderbilt.edu.udl/.

The IRIS Center Peabody College Vanderbilt University. (2016). *Perspectives and resources.* Retrieved from http://iris.peabody.vanderbilt.edu.udl/.

Jimenez, Teresa C. et al. (2007, Fall). Gaining access to general education: The promise of universal design for learning. *Issues in Teacher Education, 16*(2), 41–54.

National Governors Association and Council of Chief State School Officers. (2016). *Common Core State Standards Initiative—About the Standards.* Retrieved from http://www.corestandards.org/.

Rose, David H. (2014, July 31). *UDL Guidelines.* Retrieved from http://www.udlcenter.org/aboutudl/udlguidelines.

Rose, David H., & Gravel, Jenna. (2014, March 7). *About UDL.* Retrieved from www.udlcenter.org.

Vanderbilt University. (2016). *The IRIS Center.* Retrieved from http://iris.peabody. vanderbilt.edu/module/udl/cresource/#content.

Chapter 4

What Is Differentiated Instruction?

The success of education depends on adapting teaching to individual differences among learners.

Yuezheng, fourth century BC, in the Chinese treatise Xue Ji

Differentiated instruction is a method of instruction which can be utilized in a general education classroom to offer different approaches for different learning needs. Through differentiated instruction teachers must be prepared to address each student at their place of learning within the context of the lesson. This can include the level of learning, engagement of topic, and measure of difficulty.

As Dr. Carol Ann Tomlinson, of University of Virginia, states, the teacher must be ready to modify content and process. "Content is what (the teacher) wants the students to learn and the materials and mechanisms through which that is accomplished. Process describes activities designed to ensure that students use skills to make sense out of essential ideas and formations" (Tomlinson, 2014, p. 11).

With this in mind, modifying content and process can allow the teacher to engage all students in every lesson. Therefore, differentiated instruction allows the teacher to instruct students with disabilities, in a general education setting, through different approaches to the same concept.

To offer quality differentiated instruction, the teacher must be aware of the learning needs of all students, especially students with disabilities. Differentiated instruction allows the teacher to acknowledge that not all students are the same. They do not learn the same way, and they do not understand the same way. Differentiated instruction provides an opportunity for the teacher to respond to the individual learning of each student.

IDEA requires that students with disabilities have access to the general curriculum. These students will have a variety of learning differences that cannot be met with only one approach. One size no longer fits all, and teachers must provide multiple ways to address the needs of these students. Differentiated instruction allows the teacher to acknowledge that students grow and learn at differing rates. Each student takes their own path in learning, and when teachers provide the environment for these different paths, greater understanding takes place, especially for students with disabilities.

DIFFERENTIATED INSTRUCTION AND UNIVERSAL DESIGN FOR LEARNING

Differentiated instruction can be utilized in conjunction with universal design for learning (UDL). UDL creates the differentiated learning environments that reduce the need to modify during teaching. UDL provides the platform for differentiated instruction to take place.

UDL and differentiated instruction provide frameworks for designing curricula that enable *all* individuals to gain knowledge, skills, and enthusiasm for learning.

UDL principles assist teachers in designing instruction for a diverse group of students, while differentiated instruction principles allow them to address special skills and challenges for individual students. Therefore, UDL and differentiated instruction together allow full access to the general education curriculum as well as allow the varying abilities of students with disabilities to be recognized and addressed while maintaining high expectations for all students.

There are four areas that can be addressed within the classroom to differentiate instruction for students. These four areas rely on understanding the student's abilities, interest, and learning style. Dr. Tomlinson identifies these four areas as content, process, product, and learning environment. So when developing lessons with these four areas in mind, teachers are able to adjust the learning process by identifying the various aspects of how a student learns (Tomlinson, 2000).

Teachers can differentiate instruction through:

- Content—what the student needs to learn or how the student will get access to the information
- Process—activities in which the student engages in order to make sense of or master the content
- Products—culminating projects that ask the student to rehearse, apply, and extend what he or she has learned in a unit

- Learning environment—the way the classroom works and feels

According to the student's:

- Abilities
- Interests
- Learning styles
- Assessment

Teachers in an inclusive setting, or at least, teaching students with multiple learning issues, need to be able to teach all students in a meaningful way that meets their academic and emotional needs. Teachers need to be aware that instructional delivery must be individualized for every student, whether the student has identifiable learning needs or is just struggling with specific content.

Teachers must be aware of the students' learning needs and abilities to provide a positive learning environment. By differing the way the content is taught, the way it is accessed, and the way it is understood and demonstrated, teachers can address the learning needs of all students.

SCENARIO

Mrs. Peters teaches 6th grade. Her student teacher, Natalie, observed the language arts lesson for the day.

Mrs. Peters:	So Natalie, do you have any questions about the lesson?
Natalie:	Oh, yes, many. You did such a great job with all the students. I really liked how you seemed to understand everybody's different learning needs.
Mrs. Peters:	Well, that is one of the most important aspects of teaching, knowing your students. Instruction is not about what you are teaching, but how the students are learning.
Natalie:	Yes, I realize that is very important, but to see it in practice . . . WOW, I am not sure if I can do that.
Mrs. Peters:	You will, in time. Anyway, what about today's lesson? Shall we discuss what you observed?
Natalie:	Yes, please. So today you had the students do some work regarding the book they are reading in class. I noticed that not every student is reading the same book, why is that?
Mrs. Peters:	Well, for starters, not every student has the same interest and not every student can read at the same level. The point of the reading

is not to assess their ability to read a specific book, but to engage them in actually reading and analyzing a piece of literature. So to do that, they need to want to read the book. I let them choose from a specific list, given varying levels and interests. This approach will engage them in the lesson because they chose the book.

Natalie: Well, that certainly makes sense. So how do you develop the activities for the students to demonstrate their learning if everyone has different books and they are at different levels? I will say, I could not tell that everyone was at different levels by how hard they were working. You had everyone in centers for the second half of the period. What was that about?

Mrs. Peters: I have centers that focus on the different concepts I want them to learn. There is the writing center, spelling center, "story" center, and computer center. Each center has specific tasks for students to complete based on the content of the center. Now, not every student is doing the same thing. Based on the ability of the student, I have assigned them specific tasks that will address the area of learning I want them to achieve. After I've allowed them time to read for about 20–30 minutes, they proceed to their specific center. For example, in the writing center, there were Cindy, Shannon, Terry, and Lawrence. The writing center is where students analyze theme, plot, and make inferences of text. I have three different ways to achieve this task, depending on the level of the student. For Cindy and Lawrence, I had them draw a picture of the chapters they read today to demonstrate plot. Terry was to choose a character from his chapters and write a paragraph explaining how that character developed, or changed over time. Shannon was to use the tablet to dictate a summary of what she read. Each student was demonstrating an understanding of their reading, but through different means based on their abilities.

Natalie: WOW, I see. So each student was able to work toward the same objective, just in different ways.

Mrs. Peters: Yes, that is the point of differentiated instruction. Not all students learn the same way; therefore they must be allowed to access their learning in different ways as well.

Natalie: This definitely brings a different perspective to teaching. In my classes at the university, there has been a lot of discussion about UDL, universal design for learning. How does differentiated instruction fit in with UDL?

Mrs. Peters: That is a great question. As you may know, UDL is the design of curriculum that addresses three principles of learning, Multiple

Means of Representation, Expression, and Engagement. These three principles must be addressed throughout the unit to allow students multiple ways to access the curriculum. Now think of UDL as the umbrella, and differentiated instruction is the individual lesson under that umbrella. With UDL, you are providing different ways for the student to access the curriculum, but in differentiated instruction the student is provided ways to meet specific aspects of the lesson through targeted activities that have been determined through ongoing formative assessment. As I check for understanding through multiple means, I assign different tasks for students depending on how they are comprehending the concepts. Some concepts may come easier to some and harder for others. Depending on the abilities of the student, I differentiate how they can access the information to demonstrate learning. Does this make sense?

Natalie: Yes, UDL is developing different ways for the student to access the overall concept of the unit or standard, and differentiated instruction is the different way the student can access the objective or task.

Mrs. Peters: You could say it that way.

Natalie: Excellent. I think I see what was happening today. So at each center, you had students doing specific assignments to demonstrate understanding, based on formative assessments you have been giving throughout the unit. The assignments concentrated on specific tasks you needed them to work on, based on their level of ability.

Mrs. Peters: Yes, that is correct. I think you are beginning to understand differentiated instruction.

Natalie: Yes, I think I am as well. Thank you.

STRATEGIES FOR DIFFERENTIATED INSTRUCTION

There are multiple ways for teachers to differentiate instruction within the classroom. It can be accomplished by recognizing basic differentiated principles, providing achievable tasks, flexible grouping, formative assessment, and responding to different learning goals.

Differentiated instruction is . . .

- A teacher's response to different learning goals.
- Guided by basic differentiated principles.

- Providing achievable tasks.
- Providing flexible grouping.
- Using formative assessments with ongoing accommodations.

Examples of differentiated instruction within the classroom are stations, centers, tiered activities, small-group instruction, and teacher choice.

1. *Stations* are a form of instruction that allows for locations throughout the classroom that provide different types of activities based on a content-specific learning objective and based on student academic need. Some stations are focused toward independent learning, while others are teacher directed. Each station has different tasks for different students. Not every student needs to go to each station every day, and assignments are designed to meet the individual needs of every student.

2. *Centers* are areas in the classroom where students work independently. They are not linked by a common content area. Examples would be writing center, reading center, and math center. Centers can be defined in two different ways: either learning or interest-based. For this book, we will identify centers as learning centers, though interest centers could be considered when teaching in an inclusive setting.

   Centers are intended to develop independent learning skills while also addressing the individual learning needs of students. Centers are teacher-created. Each center is self-contained and includes the following:

   - Has clearly identifiable goals
   - Contains differing materials that allow each student to work toward the goals
   - Has range of reading and other activities to meet the goals for each student
   - Allows for a wide range of activities from simple to complex, concrete to abstract, and structured to open-ended
   - Has clear directions on how to complete the assignment, what to do when the assignment is completed, and how to ask for help when necessary
   - Has data on what and how well students completed assignment.

3. *Tiered activities* can be implemented when a concept is taught to all students, but they allow for different levels of background knowledge, comprehension, and proficiency. This approach allows all students to learn the same basic information, but accepts that students will differ in their ability to comprehend and apply the information. Providing

differing ways to approach the concept allows students to learn through their strengths, for example, developing a lesson in Addition.

INSTRUCTIONS: Identify what the student is to know: The student will calculate single/double-digit addition, up to 20.

- *Tier 1*—Student is able to add single/double-digit, up to 20, on worksheet, without manipulatives.
- *Tier 2*—Student is able to add single/double-digits, up to 20, on worksheet, using manipulatives or calculator.
- *Tier 3*—Student is able to count sets of objects, up to 20, to calculate total.

4. *Small-group instruction* is when teachers are working with small groups of students to provide re-teaching of skills or concepts, formative assessment, or target support in specific skills or lessons. The length and structure of small groups can vary and depend on the need of the students. Small groups can be part of a bigger, class rotation activity, or built into whole group instruction, when the rest of the students are working independently.

5. *Teacher choice* is used when a teacher allows for students to choose their activity from a choice board. Each student is directed to choose from a different row that is targeted to his or her specific learning need or interest. This can be used when teaching a specific subject, or for a variety of learning goals. The choices can be targeted for specific reinforcement or targeted practice of a topic. The choices are leveled to address the different needs and abilities of the students. (See figure 4.1.)

CHOICE BOARD		
Find 5 items in class that represent the number of the day.	Answer 2 of 5 Word Problems.	Draw a cartoon about the number of the day.
Write a poem using the words of the day.	Draw a picture to represent the word of the day.	Write the definitions of 5 of the 10 words on the list.
Locate the city from today's reading on a map. Find the distance from the school.	Research 3 important facts about the city from the reading.	Draw a map of where the city from the reading is located.

Figure 4.1   Choice Board

SUMMARY

Differentiated instruction is a strategy of teaching that provides a student access to the curriculum in the way that is best suited for his or her learning style. Some students are visual, others are auditory and others are kinesthetic. Whichever way is best for the student is how that student needs to learn. Not every student learns the same way. Providing different ways of accessing the curriculum is what every teacher should strive to do. It may require different approaches for different students and will allow greater opportunity of success for all students.

BIBLIOGRAPHY

Broderick, Alicia, Heeral Mehta-Parekh, & D. Kim Reid. (n.d.). Differentiating instruction for disabled students in inclusive classrooms. *Theory into Practice, 44*(3), 194–202.

Friend, Marilyn, & Bursuck, William D. (2009). *Including students with special needs: A practical guide for classroom teachers* (5th ed.). Upper Saddle River, NJ: Pearson.

Lawrence-Brown, D. (2004). Differentiated instruction: Inclusive strategies in standards-based learning that benefits the whole class. *American Secondary Education, 32*(3), 34–62.

Professional Learning Project. (n.d.). *Differentiated learning*. Retrieved from http://besplug.weebly.com/tiered-lessons.html.

Tomlinson, C.A. (2000). Differentiation of instruction in the elementary grades. *Clearinghouse on elementary and early childhood education*, 1. Retrieved from http://education.ky.gov/educational/diff/Documents/tomlin00.pdf.

Tomlinson, C.A. (2008, November). The goals of differentiation: Differentiated instruction helps students not only master content but also form their own identities as learners. *Educational Leadership*, 26. Retrieved from blogs.oregonstate.edu: blogs.oregonstate.edu/smedcohort/files/2009/10/Tomlinson-2008.PDF; http://education.ky.gov/educational/diff/Documents/tomlin00.pdf.

Tomlinson, C. A. (2014). *The differentiated classroom: Responding to the needs of all learners* (2nd ed.). Association for Supervision and Curriculum Development (ASCD) Alexandria, Virginia.

Chapter 5

What Is Formative Assessment?

Attention to minute-by-minute and day-to-day formative assessment is likely to have the biggest impact on student outcomes.

Dylan Wiliam

Formative assessment is a *process* that can be utilized to guide a teacher and student when developing lessons and understanding the needs of the student when learning a concept. Formative assessment allows the teachers to gain immediate feedback from the student and then include that information to improve the learning for the student.

Summative assessment is a *task* that occurs at the end of learning and usually results in a grade for the student. Formative assessment and summative assessment work together to allow the teacher to diagnose and prescribe accurately for every student. The preceding illustration is a simplistic way to look at the difference between formative and summative assessments. When the chef tastes the food, it's formative. When the customers taste the food, it's summative.

FORMATIVE VS. SUMMATIVE ASSESSMENT

Formative assessment happens every day in minute-by-minute and day-by-day practice. Weekly or other assessments *may* be formative *only* if teachers examine the responses and then reteach. Formative assessment is not a way to test students in the formal sense, but it is an instructional practice or process that allows for the teacher and student to interact in an ongoing discussion to fill the gap between what is taught and what needs to be learned. (See figure 5.1.)

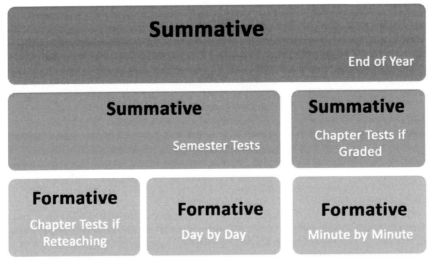

Figure 5.1   Assessment Cycle

Summative assessment happens at the end: a week, a chapter, a semester, a year, and it's usually graded. Summative assessments sum up the learning. Formative assessment is used to determine *where a student is in the learning process*. Formative assessment is not graded, but it can be marked with comments for how to improve. Figure 5.2 shows the continuous cycle of learning that occurs when formative assessment is practiced.

Figure 5.2   Learning Cycle

This cycle is repeated over and over again throughout the day, week, month, and semester. Students are made aware of where they are in the learning process and, in fact, have control over their learning. Formative assessment is also known as assessment *of* learning.

Summative assessments include end-of-the-year assessments, quarterly or trimester assessments, weekly assessments, and various teacher-designed assessments. Grades or scores are the result of summative assessments. Summative assessment is also referred to in the literature as assessment *of* learning. In summary:

- Formative assessment is assessment *for* learning
- Summative assessment is assessment *of* learning

When combined with summative assessment, formative assessment allows for student achievement, because the student knows at the end of the day what has been mastered and what needs additional focus and practice.

MISUNDERSTANDING

However, there continues to be a misunderstanding regarding formative assessment. Many teachers misuse formative assessment as an interim testing measure, and not as an instructional practice.

The core problem lies in the false, but nonetheless widespread, assumption that formative assessment is a particular kind of measurement instrument, rather than a process that is fundamental and indigenous to the practice of teaching and learning. This distinction is critical, not only for understanding how formative assessment functions, but also for realizing its promise for our students and our society (Heritage, 2010, p. 1).

Black and William in 1998 stated, "Assessment encompasses teacher observation, classroom discussion, and analysis of student work, including homework and tests. Assessments then become formative when the information is used to adapt teaching and learning to meet student needs."

Many schools think they are implementing formative assessment when they develop common interim assessments for a grade level or departments to give throughout the semester. However, *unless re-teaching occurs* or students have *the opportunity to improve their work*, these assessments are summative!

UNPACKING FORMATIVE ASSESSMENT

The literature on formative assessment refers to a five-part process that commonly refers to and includes the following practices:

1. Clarifying and Sharing Learning Intentions and Criteria for Success

Learning intentions focus on what the student will learn during one period of class. They should be clear and concise in order for students to understand what they are to learn. Learning intentions are *not* content standards. Learning intentions build on one another throughout the week to ensure students' success with a bigger concept. All students need to know the day's learning intention. Success criteria are stated at the beginning of the lesson so that students will know when the desired learning has occurred.

2. Asking Questions and Engineering Effective Classroom Discussions, Questions, and Learning Tasks That Illicit Evidence of Learning

Formative assessment questions go well beyond factual responses and lead the student to a deeper understanding. Students should be asked questions that allow for thinking and help move the learner forward in mastery. The questions should be developed in such a way that lets the teacher know immediately if students are grasping the lesson concepts. Paul Black (2003), a noted authority on formative assessment, suggests that "more effort has to be spent in framing questions that are worth asking: that is, questions which explore issues that are critical to the development of students' understanding."

Examples of effective questions for 2nd grade might be:

Content: Science Weather

Question: Which of the following are three examples of precipitation?

    A. flood, sleet, snow

    B. tornado, wind, rain

    C. *rain, hail, drizzle*

    D. mist, hurricane, puddle

The question distinguishes well between precipitation and the results/accompaniments of precipitation. Students must fully understand precipitation in order to answer the question, thus giving the teacher information on how to proceed with the lesson.

3. Giving Feedback to Move the Student Forward

Feedback needs to be specific to the assignment and something the student is able to accomplish. "Feedback designed to improve learning is more effective when it is focused on the task and provides the student with suggestions, hints, or cues, rather than offered in the form of praise or comments about performance" (Heritage, 2010, p. 5).

Comments such as "good job" or "much better" do not move the student forward because they do not let students know precisely what they are learning. Feedback that is explicit, such as "your use of descriptive words gives the reader a clear picture of the environment and the characters you are describing," provides the learner with specific information. A student then knows that using descriptive words gives the written piece more meaning to the reader, whereas "good job" keeps the student in the dark as to why the writing is good or needs changing.

4. Putting Students in Charge of Their Own Learning

In a formative assessment classroom, students are aware of where they are in their own learning. They understand the formative assessment cycle mentioned earlier, and they know what they still need to learn because learning intentions and success criteria are posted and understood by all students. Students are engaged in doing better through the questions asked by the teacher. They are able to redo assignments, ask questions of the teacher and peers to better understand the content, and know where to go for help or assistance.

As one teacher shared, "Learning intentions are a regular part of our day now. We regularly check back during the day to see if we have met them. The students are paying closer attention in lessons."

5. Activating Students as Instructional Resources for One Another

Students act as resources for each other in order to activate learning. This can be cooperative learning, paired learning, or acting as an expert for other students. When students become instructional resources for one another, they strengthen their own learning and the student they are helping. Often the help of a peer is more valuable to the student because they feel more comfortable asking the embarrassing questions.

Students helping students is a powerful tool to use for students with disabilities or second-language learners, because they may not have the skills to speak out in front of the whole class or may be too shy to ask the teacher for further explanation.

In one 1st-grade classroom, a teacher had one highly gifted student and several students with disabilities. The teacher had the gifted student research and present additional support material to the students with disabilities about the subject of birds that correlated with a story they were going to read in class. The gifted student was given a differentiated assignment that allowed the students with disabilities to hear from a peer and be able to understand the subject better. It was a win-win situation for all of the students involved. This is definitely a tool you want to use often!

Formative assessments can be implemented as an instructional practice with both students in general and special education classes as a way to evaluate the student's progress toward gaining understanding of the academic concepts presented prior to needing to be at mastery. The teacher can use the information to reteach, try alternative approaches, or offer more time for practice so the student can succeed.

SCENARIO

Theresa was looking at her lesson plan and trying to figure out how to accommodate her two full-inclusion 7th-grade students into tomorrow's discussion. They had been struggling of late and finding it difficult to keep up. Then she remembered a session she had attended at the conference on working with students with disabilities and formative assessment. Pulling out her notes and handouts she decided to seek assistance from the special education teacher, Loryn.

Theresa: Hi Loryn, I hope you can help me with something to assist my two students who are fully included.

Loryn: I'd love to help you. What are you and they struggling with in your class?

Theresa: Well, we are beginning a new unit in social studies, and I've noticed they are really struggling. There is so much reading and conceptual understanding that they need to accomplish.

Loryn: I see you have some information on formative assessment. Do you want to explore using this process?

Theresa: I went to a session on it at the beginning of the year and now I'm curious if it can help!

Loryn: There are five strategies in formative assessment. Let's look at your notes and see which of the strategies is better for your students.

Looking at notes and handouts

Loryn: Let's tackle the reading issue first. One of the strategies is for students to act as resources for each other. Are you comfortable with having students work together? One student could read the assignment out loud for your students who are fully included.

Theresa: Yes, I could arrange for that to happen. Is there something else in the notes that would be good for the students?

Loryn: Let's take a look. As I mentioned, there are five strategies. One is clarifying learning intentions and providing success criteria, another is providing clear feedback with specific information. Then there is students responsible for their own learning, but I really think questioning is another place to begin. If you implement a think, pair, share technique your students would have the benefit of others' thinking. Every time you ask a question, pause for 30 seconds so the students all have time to think of an answer. Then have them pair to talk about the appropriate answer. You can then call on several students before calling on one of your two students who are fully included. That way they have several chances to hear answers. You can ask each student to expand on another student's answer. I think these two formative assessments will definitely work!

Theresa: Thank you so much for your assistance. Let's meet in a couple of days so I can be sure I am on the right track.

STRATEGIES FOR FORMATIVE ASSESSMENT

There are many examples of formative assessment strategies in the literature, on the web, and in books. Here you will find a sample of some techniques that you will find successful. It is important to remember not to implement too many at one time. Practically speaking, do not try to implement more than two at a time. Once you have mastered two, you can refer back to this list and find another that works with your teaching style. If you try one and it doesn't feel comfortable for you, discard it and try another. The techniques are listed under the five general strategies of formative assessment.

1. Clarifying learning intentions and success criteria
   * *Learning intentions* are very specific statements of the day's expected learning. Learning intentions need to be valuable to learn, concise in wording, and clear for the learner to understand. Learning intentions should be posted new every day. The teacher begins the lesson by going over the learning intentions and ends the lesson by reviewing the learning intentions for mastery by the students. This before and after process is important for students to clearly understand what is expected of them. An example of a clear, concise, and valuable

learning intention is: "I will know how to divide a whole number by another whole number without a remainder."

- *Success criteria* tell students how to be successful in the day's task. Taking the example of the learning intention earlier, students will know that when all of the problems given to them are completed without ending up with a remainder they are successful. So the success criteria would be "Check your partner's problems. They should be correct answers with no remainder."

- *Keyword posters* are developed for the day's work with the academic vocabulary words listed. The definitions may or may or not be on the poster. An example of a keyword poster is in Appendix A. A keyword poster allows the students to have an introduction to the important words they should master and/or define during the lesson. It gives them a head's up to what is coming. The teacher reviews each of the words on the poster and, depending on whether it is a new word or a review word, will give the definition to the students or call on students to give the definition.

- *Rubrics* used in formative assessment are a set of guidelines given to students to promote the consistent application of learning intentions in the classroom, or to measure their mastery of academic success. They are the success criteria given in advance of an assignment. Rubrics help to ensure consistency in the evaluation of academic work from student to student, assignment to assignment, or course to course. Rubrics may be provided and explained to students before they begin an assignment to ensure that learning intentions have been clearly communicated to and understood by students. Giving students a rubric allows them to be responsible for their learning. It tells them exactly what needs to be in the assignment. Students don't have to wonder. Rubrics are especially helpful to students with disabilities so they don't have to guess how good is good enough. It's right in the rubric for them (Appendices B/C).

- *Sharing exemplars of student work* is an excellent way for students to *see* what it is they are supposed to be accomplishing. Each year save a few examples of the outstanding work to show the next year's class. These exemplar papers or projects work nicely with rubrics. Some teachers choose to save work at all levels of a rubric in order for students to see in advance what a 1, 2, 3, or 4 paper or project looks like. You always want students to strive for their best, so it will be important for you to explain clearly what the attributes of the paper or project are that resulted in the final score. Of course, with all things formative, the student must have the opportunity to continue working toward the highest score possible through rewrites and so on.

2. Giving feedback to move the student forward
   - *Two stars and a wish* is a process where the teacher or fellow students look at student's work and highlight two areas of mastery and one area that needs improvement. For example, a 6th-grade class is working on ancient world cultures and the students have been asked to select one of the cultures presented to date and write what has been learned about that culture. The paper may be presented to the entire class, given to one student to review, or to a small group of students. Using their notes and textbook, they review the writing and elicit two ideas that are strongly presented and one idea that may be a little weak and needs more detail by the student (see Appendix D).

   - *Find and correct errors* is a great formative assessment to use with students with disabilities or if you want to differentiate. If a practice sheet of math problems has been given as an assignment, the teacher may say to one student who is more proficient to review all of the problems and find the two that are wrong. For the slightly struggling student, the teacher may say, "Look at row 3 and find the one problem with the wrong answer and correct it." For a more struggling student the teacher may be more specific and say, "One of these two problems is wrong. Can you find it and correct it." Find and correct errors allows for differentiation and gives the teacher valuable information on how well a student really understands the concept presented.

   - *Reach for the next level* allows the teacher to stretch students. If for instance a student receives a 2 on a 4-point rubric, the teacher can be very specific as to what has to change for the student to reach for the next level. With specific information, students do not have to guess, but rather can build confidence in their ability to learn because they understand what to change.

   - *Strategy cards/stickers* are premade cards or stickers that highlight a concept to be learned. For instance, a teacher is focusing on placing appropriate capital letters in written work and a student fails to apply the strategy. The teacher may clip or stick on the paper a premade comment that may say, "Please review your writing and place capital letters on appropriate words such as, people, places or things." The strategy cards allow the teacher to move more quickly through the review process of student work and allow students important feedback to gain mastery of their learning.

- *Comment-only marking* is an important part of formative assessment. Since grades are not given and students are still in the learning phase, specific comments by the teacher as mentioned earlier in this chapter are critical for improvement. A primary child doesn't understand "good work" and a middle or high school student doesn't understand what "nice try" means. Specific comments such as "Can you tell me more about your main Character" or "Your long division numerals are not in columns so it makes it difficult to understand how you solved these problems. Please redo, being careful to use vertical columns to show your work. You may use graph paper if that will help you with alignment."

3. Asking questions and engineering effective classroom discussions, questions, and learning tasks that elicit evidence of learning

   - *Diagnostic questions* let the teacher know at any time in the lesson if the students are mastering the concept. Diagnostic questions should be deeper than recall questions, for example, When water droplets appear on the outside of a glass of ice water, where do the droplets come from?
     - They leak through the pores in the glass
     - The glass is sweating
     - From water vapor in the surrounding air
     - From the ice changing state from a solid

     This is a great question as it gets at common student misconceptions and allows for rich discussion possibilities. By discussing each possible answer after students select the one they think is correct, the teacher engages students of all learning abilities and is able to discern who is still having difficulty with the concept.

   - *ABCD cards* are one of the easiest formative assessment techniques to implement. Look at the preceding question in diagnostic questions. Students would have separate cards with A, B, C, and D on their desks. When the question is shown either on the board or electronically, students determine their answer and hold the card close to their chest so others cannot see what they selected. When all cards are on chests, the teacher asks them to hold them up. Right away the teacher can see every student and what each student selected as the answer. The teacher does not give the correct answer at this point. If there are multiple answers, the teacher then asks students why they selected "A," "B," "C," or "D." Then teacher asks if anyone wants to change their answer after hearing from multiple students. Once the final answers are held up, the teacher is able to see immediately who needs re-teaching and who has fairly mastered the concept of precipitation. If everyone has the correct answer, the teacher can go on with the planned lesson. If a large group of students need re-teaching, it is easier to reteach the entire class or use those who answered correctly to work as peer teachers with the students needing assistance (see Appendices E/F).

- *Whiteboards* are in many classrooms already, so it's time to put them to good use, especially with students with disabilities. Similar to the ABCD cards, a whiteboard allows the teacher to see everyone's answer at once. An effective adaptation of these techniques is to have students pair up and explain their answers to each other before holding them up for the teacher to see. This adaptation allows students with disabilities to be paired with a more knowledgeable student on the particular content and give time for extra instruction.

- *No hands up: Popsicle® sticks/call sticks* are used in many primary classrooms. Upper and middle School teachers often use 3 × 5 cards instead. Both are effective and it is left up to you as the teacher to decide which one to use. Put all the students' names on a separate stick or card. Ask a question, and wait 30 seconds so all of the students have time to think of an answer. Then pull a stick or a card and ask the student whose name is on the stick or card to respond. If the student has difficulty, pick another stick or card and ask the second student to answer. Then go back to the first student and ask that student to paraphrase the correct answer that the second student offered. An adaptation is to ask the class if the student gave the correct answer. If not, why not? Continue using the sticks or cards to call on students. The key to using this strategy is to be sure and put the student's stick or card back in the can or pile. By doing this, students are on notice that they may be called on again (and probably will be if chance is in play).

  This technique is excellent for students with disabilities. First, they realize they must be listening; second, if they don't know an answer and are called on, there is no penalty. A second student or a third or fourth gives the answer and then they are called on again to paraphrase or repeat verbatim. Always remember to go back to the students who could not answer so that they realize they will be held accountable.

- *Exit tickets* are a way for teachers to get a quick response to an important question from all students. Before the period or class is over, pose an important question that can be answered briefly. It might be a mathematical problem, a word problem, or another type of question. Before students are able to leave or change to another subject they must answer the question on a 3 × 5 card. The teacher can rapidly go through the cards and see where the next day's lesson must begin.

- *Responders* are electronic devices connected to computers in the class-room. Similar to the ABCD cards, responders allow the teacher to ask a question with multiple choice answers, the students then reply on their responder whether the answer is A, B, C, or D (or more choices if preferred). Programs allow the answers to be anonymous, or the teacher may want to input student names. It is a novel way for students to respond and remain engaged. Teachers may pair a student with a student with a disability, and the two students would respond as one.

4. Putting students in charge of their own learning

- *Stop/slow signals* are colored disks or plastic cups of red, green, and yellow. Students determine, as the lesson proceeds, whether they understand (green cup or disk is displayed), are not quite sure of what they are doing (yellow cup or disk is displayed), or are completely lost (red cup or disk is displayed). These signals may be used during a directed lesson, independent work time, or collaborative group time. For younger students it is advisable to use just a green or red until they can manage efficiently. The use of stop / slow signals is twofold. The teacher can see immediately who needs help, and students begin to take responsibility for acknowledging what they know and what they don't know. The key to the success of this technique is to notice when a student has changed the color from green to either yellow or red. It takes some practice in the beginning, but once it becomes a habit, students begin to be more honest about where they are in their learning.

- *Self-evaluation rubric* is similar to a rubric one might use as success criteria, but it allows the students to reflect on mastery of their learning. For younger students it may be as simple as "I put capital letters on all the persons, places or things that should have them," with an "always," "mostly," or "never." For older students, they would be asked to use the grading rubric and evaluate their own assignment before turning it in. Students would then be given time to make the necessary changes, ask for help, or review sources before turning in the assignment.

- *Question strips* are simple and easy to implement. Cut 8½ × 11 copy paper into six strips. Place a pile of the strips in an area that is easy for students to access. If desks are in groups, the strips could be in the middle. If individual desks, give each student 10 or so strips. Let them know that they are to write down any questions they made need answers to in the lesson or if they need more information.

    For instance, a student might write "Can you review the reasons for the Westward Movement again?" or "Will you explain how to turn fractions into decimals?" This technique is excellent for middle and high schools where students may be too embarrassed to ask a question aloud. It is also helpful in group work, where a struggling student or student with disabilities may not want attention, but really needs to have something reviewed.

Students put the anonymous strips in a basket or may leave them on their desks. The teacher retrieves them and determines the best time to go over the question with the entire class. Many older students will never ask for an explanation, but the anonymity of question strips gives them confidence to ask.

- *Pre-flight checklist* is exactly what a pilot goes through prior to flying an aircraft. It is a list for students to review prior to attempting an independent project or assignment. It could be for younger students as simple as:

1. I have a pencil to do my work.
2. I have the right worksheet or paper.
3. I know when it needs to be finished.
4. I know where to put the paper when finished.
5. I know what to do when I finish my work, I will _____.

Or for older students:

1. I know what my assignment is for tomorrow.
2. I know what resources I need to complete the assignment.
3. I have enough time scheduled to complete the assignment.
4. I need to read the following pages in order to complete the assignment_____.

If students are completing a report, the pre-flight checklist could include the parts of the report they will need to include:

1. Title page
2. Introduction
3. Five paragraph or five concept explanation
4. Conclusion
5. Summary
6. Bibliography or resources used

Just think about the thinking that must go into completing a pre-flight checklist. It grounds the student in the learning and the task. For a student with disabilities, organization is often an issue. The pre-flight checklist allows them to understand prior to beginning the assignment what resources need to be available. Some teachers develop one pre-flight checklist that they use all year-long. Others develop a new pre-flight checklist for each major task. The choice is yours to make. Make it your preflight checklist simple and make it so students will move their learning forward and accomplish the task required.

- *Traffic lighting self* is an adaptation to the stop and slow signals. The teacher gives the students a list of topics that are required for mastery of the content. Students then evaluate their own knowledge by marking a green, yellow, or red mark or sticker by each topic. The teacher may have each student complete the traffic lighting self individually or make a poster with the topics and throughout the period/day; students go up and make a green, yellow, or red mark by the collective poster. By the end of the period/day, the teacher can see at a glance where students are having difficulty and students learn by repeating this process over and over and that they will get the help they need, but they must be honest about their learning (see Appendix G).

5. Activating students as instructional resources for one another

- *Think/pair/share* was mentioned earlier in the chapter. The teacher asks a question, gives students time to think of their answer, and then pairs up students with other students to discuss their answers. Finally, the teacher calls on students to share their answers. (See figure 5.3.)

THINK
Students think about a response to a question

PAIR
Students share with a partner their answer

SHARE
Students share their work with the class

Figure 5.3   Think/Pair/Share

- *Carousel* is a technique that allows for group work and allows the teacher to see and understand the students' thinking. Students respond to a question or questions on chart paper that is placed around the room. After all students respond, they carousel from chart to chart adding information or placing question marks (??) for further explanation. The teacher or a student then reads the content on the chart, posing any questions that have arisen for the class to answer. (See figure 5.4.)

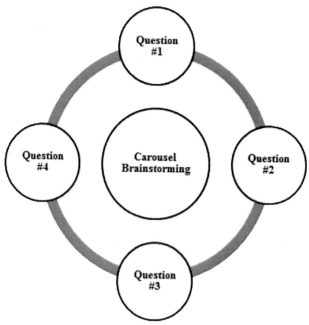

Figure 5.4 Carousel Brainstorming

- *Partner learning* is a time-saving and valuable way for students to learn. In pairs, students are given a specific issue, question, or problem to solve. They are given a set amount of time to work on the problem before the teacher asks for students to share out to the entire class. Students have the opportunity to learn from a peer in language that is different from the teacher's.

- *Homework help board* provides students with help the morning after the homework was to be completed, but before it needs to be handed in. At a designated spot in the room, the teacher posts a "homework help" sign.

Students who feel confident about their homework can stand or sit near the sign and be available for students having difficulty. The one rule is that the confident student cannot "give" the answer to the student having difficulty. The confident student must reteach the concept and help the student figure out where the difficulty lies.

- *Evaluation with rubrics* is a key strategy for use with upper elementary, middle, and high school students. Given a rubric before the lesson begins allows the student to understand the important learning target. As students complete the assignment, they can evaluate each other and themselves against the rubric prior to turning in the assignment.

- *Jigsaw* is a strategy akin to cooperative learning. Students are grouped together either heterogeneously or homogeneously. The group is given a selection to read. Each member, however, only has to read a portion of the selection. After a designated amount of time for reading silently, the students share in sequence what they read while the other students in the group listen and take notes, thus providing students an opportunity to become an expert and to actively help each other build comprehension. (See figure 5.5.)

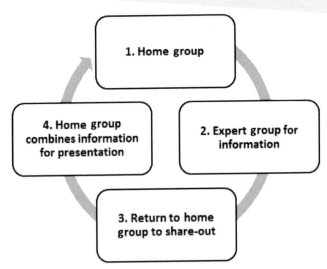

Figure 5.5   Jigsaw

This is an excellent process to use with students with disabilities. You can pair a student with another student to read their part out loud and then let the student with disabilities be the expert who shares the information.

SUMMARY

Formative assessment works! Besides the resources mentioned next, there are hundreds of scholarly articles on the success of formative assessment. It allows teachers and students to know where they are in the learning process minute-by-minute and day-by-day. Students become more confident learners, and teachers become more knowledgeable of their students' progress toward today's rigorous standards. It's a win-win situation, so give it a try and see how your classroom changes for the good.

BIBLIOGRAPHY

Black, P. (2003). Assessment for Learning, McGraw-Hill Education, U.K.

Black, P., & Wiliams, D. (2001). *Inside the black box—Raising standards through classroom assessment.* London: King's College, School of Education.

Black, P., & Wiliams, D. (2001). *Inside the black box—Raising standards through classroom assessment.* London: King's College, School of Education.

Chappuis, J. (2009). *Seven strategies of assessment for learning.* Education Testing Service Portland, Oregon.

Dyer, K. (2013). *Formative assessment works—Two research-based proof points make the case.* Retrieved from https://www,nwea,org/blog/2013/formative-assessment-works-two-research-based-proof-points-make-case.

Heritage, M. (2010, September). *Formative assessment and next-generation assessment systems: Are we losing on opportunity?* University of California, Los Angeles, School of Education and Information Studies.

National Center for Research on Evaluation, Standards and Student Testing. (2006). *Keeping learning on track.* Educational Testing Service. Princeton, New Jersey

Stiggins, R. (2006, November/December). *Assessment for learning, A key to motivation and achievement.* Edge: Assessment for Learning.

Stiggins, R., Arter, J.A., Chappuis, J., & Chappius, S. (2006). *Classroom assessment for student learning.* Educational Testing Service. Princeton, New Jersey

What Is Formative Assessment? (2016). Retrieved from http://www.nctm.org/Research-and-Advocacy/research-brief-and-clips/Benefits-of-Formative Assessment.

Wylie, C., & Lyon, C. (2012, June). Formative assessment—Supporting students' learning. *R and D Connections, 19,* pp. 1–12.

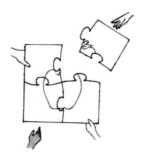

Chapter 6

What Is Cooperative Learning?

When you include the extremes of everybody, that's to say differently abled people of all sorts, then you produce things that are better for all of us.

Michael Wolff, Wolff Olins

Cooperative learning has been an instructional strategy since the 1980s. It has taken many forms and has been used in multiple ways through the years. Spencer Kagan states it simply: "Cooperative Learning involves small groups of students working cooperatively in teams toward academic goals" (Zahn, Kagan, & Widaman, 1986).

Cooperative learning can be any activity that requires two or more students to work together toward a common goal. For an inclusive classroom technique, cooperative learning can be implemented to engage students with disabilities in a small-group setting, working with different students in the class. Cooperative learning techniques can be used in multigrade classrooms, mixed ability and skill levels. Each student is able to work at their level, contributing to the common set goal for the group to succeed.

An example of cooperative learning is peer-tutoring. Peer-tutoring allows students with and without disabilities to engage in academic activities within the general education classroom. Peer-tutoring can be implemented with same-age or cross-age students, students with and without disabilities, as well as students with varying degrees of disabilities tutoring each other.

Peer-tutoring activities are very effective in engaging students in either a general or special education classroom. Activities that are well structured are highly effective in allowing all students to engage in a lesson at their abilities while interacting appropriately with their peers. It also allows students to work together in a more inclusive environment.

For an inclusive classroom, cooperative learning has many benefits, both socially and academically. It allows for differing levels of students to be resources for each other, as well as allow students of all abilities to engage in common activities, equally. The differences between the students fade as a genuine relationship of equality emerges. With such a wide range of students within an inclusive classroom, ensuring that students with learning issues share their expertise with the other students in the group makes for an equal balance within the classroom setting.

SCENARIO 1

Cooperative Learning in an Inclusive Classroom

Jill is a teacher at ABC elementary school. She has 25 3rd- and 4th-grade students with academic abilities ranging from gifted to severe learning disabilities. She has five students on IEPs, and three students on 504s for extended time on assignments. She co-teaches with the special education teacher, Sarah, for reading and math three days a week. On the other two days, Jill struggles to develop lessons for all the students to access. Even with UDL principles in place, she knows that she needs more time to spend with the students with lower academic abilities. She discusses the issue with her principal, Dr. James, and Sarah.

Jill:	Dr. James, I just don't know about all the levels of students in my class. I feel good about the progress we can make when Sarah is with me, but the other two days I feel like the class is just treading water. I can't reach all the students and make sure they understand the information. Plus, with some of the students needing extra time on the assignments, my higher academic students are sitting and waiting, or I have them do extra work, which really is not fair to them.
Sarah:	Have you thought about working in small groups with the students needing extra help and having the higher-achieving students work independently?
Jill:	I have tried that on some occasions; however, the higher-achieving students still finish early and need something to do.
Dr. James:	Jill, I understand the problem you are having. Are you saying you want all students engaged for the same length of time, being productive and learning?
Jill:	Yes. I want a way to engage all students, at a high cognitive level of thinking that does not require some students doing extra work to stay engaged, while waiting for others.

Dr. James: Have you thought of incorporating cooperative learning for your class? It can be very successful in an inclusive classroom.

Jill: What kind of cooperative learning? I am not sure. How would that work?

Dr. James: Well, after you introduce a topic to the class, you place students in pairs or quads, making sure there is a high academic student, and a lower academic student in each pair or group. The students work on the topic together. The students are engaged while you circulate to make sure all students are sharing and learning. This also allows you the ability to provide the extra time some students need to comprehend and finish the work.

Sarah: Oh, that would be great! I have read that this type of approach works perfectly in an inclusive classroom. The higher-achieving students are more engaged in the topic because they gain a sense of responsibility toward the other students, and all the students are more engaged because they are learning while interacting with their peers.

Jill: How do I group them?

Sarah: It is up to you. There are different ways. You can group by levels such as high and low academic levels. Within the groups, it is good to have different roles of leadership. Such as leader, note-taker, time keeper's. This allows each person to have a purpose within the group. It is good to change the roles frequently so everyone gets a chance to do something different, and the higher academic students are not always feeling "put upon" to be the leaders. It also gives the lower academic students a chance to be the leader sometimes. You would just have to observe and then step in when necessary.

Jill: I like this idea. The students would need to be taught how to work effectively though.

Dr. James: Yes there would have to be initial training and planning involved, but eventually, the students would get the hang of it.

Sarah: You know, you could also ask Dave S., the 5th-grade teacher, if he had some students who would like to come in and assist on those days. This could be a great way to collaborate on some cross-age tutoring projects.

Jill: Yes, that would be great during certain units that are coming up.

Dr. James: So Jill does this help you with your current classroom issue?

Jill: Yes, thank you both. I will try it.

SCENARIO 2

Peer Buddy Program to Promote Acceptance in Segregated School

Jessica P. is a special education teacher at a K–6th-grade elementary school. She teaches 3rd–6th-grade students in an SDC moderate/severe disabilities classroom. This is her second year at the school, and her classroom is at the end of the hall next to the K–2 SDC classroom. Jessica P. really wants to have her students more involved in the campus community.

Right now, they are rarely included in the general education activities, and there is limited integration among the students in her class and with their grade-level peers. Also, the students from the general education classrooms are not very friendly and often make fun of the students from her class. She is seeking a way to change the perception of her students and have them feel more included within the school community.

Her principal, Dr. Peters, is also in his second year at the school. He has seen the segregation of the students in the SDC and wants to change the perception as well. He meets with Jessica P. and the lead upper-grade teacher, Bob J., to discuss what can be done.

Dr. Peters:	Thank you Jessica and Bob for coming in today. I wanted to continue our discussion we had at lunch about developing a way to have the students in our general education program stop teasing the students in your class, Jessica. I am very concerned about the behavior of the students during lunch and on the playground.
Jessica:	So am I. It is making recess a very scary place for some the students from my classroom.
Bob:	I know, I have seen it myself. I have talked with the other teachers about this. We have all talked to our students, but it hasn't seemed to be effective.
Dr. Peters:	What can we do? We have to change their perception of the students in your class Jessica. Make them see that they are not as different as they think. We need to have them see them as just any other student at this school.
Jessica:	Well, I do have an idea, but it would require planning with the upper-grade teachers and instruction time in the day.
Dr. Peters:	How much instruction time?
Bob:	What kind of additional planning?
Jessica:	Well, what we need is an opportunity for the students from general education to interact with the students from my class. What

if we planned, say 30 minutes, 3–4 days a week where some students from the upper grades came into the SDC class and worked with the students. They could do reading, academics, maybe some functional skill activities. The students from general education would be "helping" the students in my class on how to complete tasks or they could read to them and ask questions for comprehension, or just do a fun art activity and engage them in conversation or something similar.

Bob: That sounds good, but where are we getting this extra 30 minutes to implement it?

Dr. Peters: Doesn't upper grade have a rotation after lunch for the students to choose an "elective" activity?

Bob: Yes, but how would that work?

Dr. Peters: What if we have the SDC class as a choice for the other students. It could be like a peer-tutoring opportunity. Only a few students would go at a time, and Jessica could plan with the other upper-grade teachers what kinds of activities coordinate with your program.

Bob: OK, this could work. It would be a great opportunity for the students to see what your class is like and hopefully learn to interact with the students in a positive way.

Dr. Peters: Jessica, if you like this idea, let's see if we can't get students to you by Monday.

Bob: How many peer tutors would you want Jessica?

Jessica: Oh, maybe 5–6. They need to have good, positive behaviors and not behind in academics. I know that one of the rotations you have is study skills, and I don't want their grades to be suffering. These will be the ambassadors of the school, all others will be looking to them and watching how they interact. They have to want to work with the students as well.

Bob: OK, we will ask for volunteers at first, but if this takes off, we will need to develop a more structured way to proceed.

Dr. Peters: Agreed. Thank you.

STRATEGIES FOR COOPERATIVE LEARNING

1. *Jigsaw* is a cooperative learning technique teaching students that they are one piece of the whole picture. Students begin in a "home group" of

students. They are then chosen to be in an "expert group" to work with other students on the same topic. Once they have gathered their information, they return to their home group to share what they learned with the others. As a home group, they combine their information to create a completed project with all relevant information obtained. The jigsaw technique helps students realize they are necessary pieces of a whole and encourages cooperation in a sharing, learning environment. This is also considered a formative assessment technique.

2. *Think-pair-share* is an excellent formative assessment and cooperative learning technique for students to partner with each other during a direct-instruction lesson. Upon teacher prompt, students think to themselves about a topic and then pair with another student to discuss their thoughts. The pair then shares their thoughts with the rest of the class. This technique encourages independent thinking, facilitates teamwork, and allows students to revise their thoughts before sharing with the whole class.

3. *Numbered heads together* is a different approach to whole-class question and answer. In the numbered heads together approach, the students are in groups of 3–4. The teacher numbers off the students within the group (e.g., 1–4), and then asks a question. Within the group the students "put their heads together" to develop a complete answer to the question. The teacher calls a number, and the student with that number raises his or her hand to answer the question. Since the group developed the answer, all students know the answer. It allows for individual accountability while allowing for collaborative work. This is also considered a formative assessment technique.

4. *Three-step interview* is a cooperative learning technique that allows for partner work within a larger group setting. Two students within the group interview each other. They, in turn, share with the larger group what they learned about their partner. All students share, and it promotes good listening and communication skills.

5. *Round robin* is a simple way for students to share information within a small group. Students take turns sharing information with their group. The teacher then has the group report out in either oral or written format. This is considered a formative assessment technique.

6. *Inside-outside circle* can be a fun, interactive, technique that allows all levels of learners to interact equally. Students stand in two circles, one inside the other. With prompted questions/note cards, students ask and respond to each other in a set amount of time. When told to move, the students move one person and ask another question. When time is done,

each student has spoken to every student. They students share information and teach each other at the same time.

7. *Roundtable* is a simple cooperative learning activity that has students working together on the same project. Each student contributes information to the same paper as it is passed around the group. It can be effective with brainstorming and writing activities.

SUMMARY

Cooperative learning is a teaching technique that requires some preparation but can be incorporated in any classroom for any content. It allows all students to interact equally and be a part of a group that is working together for the same goal. It can be implemented for small discussion or for big projects. Either way, it allows students to be equal in their learning and equal among their peers.

BIBLIOGRAPHY

Coffey, H. (n.d.). *Cooperative learning.* Retrieved from http://www.learnnc.org/lp/pages/4653.

Cooper-Duffy, D. M. (2003). Evidence-based practices for students with severe disabilities and the requirement for accountability in "No Child Left Behind." *The Journal of Special Education, 37*(3), 157–163. doi: 10.1177/00224669030370030501.

Jimenez, Terese C. et al. (2007). Gaining access to general education: The promise of universal design for learning. *Issues in Teacher Education, 16*(2), 41–54.

Johnson, R. T. (1994). An overview of cooperative learning. In A. V. J. Thousand (Ed.), *Creativity and Collaborative Learning.* Baltimore, MD: Brookes Press.

Terese C. Jimenez, et al. (2007). Gaining access to general education: The promise of universal design for learning. *Issues in Teacher Education, 16*(2), 41–54.

Vaughn, A. G. (2000, March). Planning for the inclusive classroom: Meeting the needs of diverse learners. *Catholic Education: A Journal of Inquiry and Practice, 3*(3), 363–375.

Zahn, L. G., Kagan, S., & Widaman, K. F. (1986). Cooperative learning and classroom climate. *Journal of School Psychology, 24,* 351–362.

Chapter 7

What Is Assistive Technology?

For people without disabilities, technology makes things easier. For people with disabilities, technology makes things possible.

IBM Training Manual, 1991

Now that we have discussed the inclusionary and instructional strategies for students with disabilities, we need to discuss how they will access the curriculum. Some students will need some form of technology to help them access the content. So what is assistive technology? Assistive technology is the use of any form of equipment, used by students to improve their ability to access and participate in their education. For example, a nonverbal student might utilize a tablet to communicate through a speech application.

Assistive technology devices are utilized by a single student to allow greater access, as well as provide the ability to participate in his or her educational program more successfully. The student with the tablet can now participate in a lesson by responding to the teacher and peers using the assigned assistive technology device. Assistive technology is defined in IDEA 2004 as "any item, piece of equipment, or product system, whether acquired commercially, off the shelf, modified, or customized, that is used to increase, maintain, or improve functional capabilities of a child with a disability."

There are multiple forms of technology that students can use to access the curriculum. Some devices can be very complex (high-tech), and others can be very simple (low-tech), depending on the needs of the student. There are also web-based and non-web-based tools for students to access.

The severity of the disability will dictate the type of technology needed to allow access. However, some students *may not require* assistive technology, but could benefit from it as it would enhance their engagement in the curriculum. For classroom instruction, there are a few universal technology tools that can be used to include all students, especially students with disabilities. Figure 7.1 gives examples of various tools for students to use within the classroom.

	Web-Based	Non-Web-Based	High-Tech	Low-Tech
Smartboard®	X		X	
Tablet	X			X
Text-to-speech apps.	X			X
Scribing pens	X			X
Keyboards		X		X
Proloque2® (speech app)	X		X	
Go-Talk® (speech device)		X		X
Large monitor screens (visual impairment)		X		X
Hearing amplification devices		X	X	X

Figure 7.1   Assistive Technology

SMART Board® technologies, tablets, and iPods® are some of the universal devices provided by school districts to all students to allow greater access to general education curriculum. Technology makes accessing curriculum possible for students with disabilities. It is important that educators consider all factors when determining the best technology for students with disabilities. The tool has to be accessible and easily manageable. Understanding the purpose and how it will be used is crucial to the success of the student. Assistive technology becomes a useless tool if it is not appropriate for the needs of the student. Proper selection and implementation is necessary for the assistive technology device to be useful.

In a classroom setting, the education professionals, or individual educational plan (IEP) team, must identify the needs of the student and then provide the assistive technology item at no cost. These assistive technology items are intended for the functional use of the student to provide greater access to school, home, and community.

For example, when a student with a fine motor disability is required to write a summary of the text just read, instead of struggling to write with pen and paper, the student can dictate the summary into the tablet, see what he or she dictated, make grammatical corrections where necessary, and then send the assignment to the teacher electronically. The student has met the goal of the assignment, without being penalized for the disability. The student had access to the curriculum through different means and did not limit his or her ability to engage in the assignment.

SCENARIO 1

Accessing Curriculum

Abby, a 7th-grade English teacher, has three students in her class with IEPs: Peter, Jeff, and Suzy. Each student has a significant cognitive delay. However, they are able to participate in the class lessons with support.

As the year progressed, however, and the curriculum became more demanding, she noticed that the three students were not able to "keep up" academically with the other students during writing lessons. Their expressive language skills were not at the same functioning level as the other students in the class. She knew the students were engaged and wanted to share their thoughts, but written language was still a struggle and hindered their ability to participate with the whole class. They needed more and more individualized instruction and less participation with the whole group. The class paraprofessional, Mr. George, was pulling them more and more to help with the writing lessons. This began to concern Abby. She consulted with the special education teacher, Catherine, to see how this could be addressed in the class.

Abby:	Catherine, I wanted to ask for your advice on three students in the class. I am concerned with the lack of progress Peter, Jeff, and Suzy are making in writing. Although I know they are engaged with the topic, they are not able to write at the same pace as the rest of the class. Mr. George has to pull them almost every day to help with their writing. This is causing them to fall behind in the other assignments. I need some suggestions on what to do.
Catherine:	Well, what exactly is the writing assignment about?
Abby:	The lesson is for the students to write a paragraph addressing the day's topic. We are working a five-sentence paragraph, highlighting key ideas, with an opening and closing sentence.
Catherine:	OK, what is the issue with the three students?
Abby:	They are not able to write the paragraph. They tell me their ideas but cannot write the words. They have difficulty spelling and remembering the correct grammar and punctuation. They are not able to

produce a paragraph within the time of the class. Mr. George has to help them with every word, with spelling and sentence structure.

Catherine: Yes, I can see this would be frustrating. Now you say they can tell you their ideas? When they tell you, does it sound like a good paragraph? Does what they are saying have structure?

Abby: Yes, for the most part, but they are not able to write it down after that.

Catherine: Do they have to write it down? Is that the point of the assignment?

Abby: I am teaching writing. I am willing to be flexible, but they do need to know how to write a paragraph.

Catherine: I am not disagreeing with you, but maybe there is another way to have them produce the paragraph. Have you heard of Dragon Dictation®?

Abby: No, I have not. What is it?

Catherine: It is an app that can be downloaded to a tablet. The students can dictate their ideas and the app will record and display what they said. Then, the students can correct the grammar, punctuation, and sentence structure directly on the tablet. They can then print out their paragraph. If the handwriting is what is holding them back, then let's take that out as an obstacle. They will still be correcting their grammar and spelling, as well as addressing their sentence and paragraph structure.

Abby: WOW, that sounds like a great idea. I can allow them to dictate in the back of the room, as to not disturb the others, but then come right back to their desk to edit. This will also allow me to help them and address any issues and Mr. George can help other students as well. Thank you.

Catherine: I will come by tomorrow during your English class to make sure the programs are set up and work with them the first few times. We want the students to feel comfortable with process.

Abby: Thank you again.

SCENARIO 2

Communication

Cindy, a 6th-grade teacher, has a student, Kelly, with an IEP. The student's main disability is communication disorder. Kelly works with the school's speech and language pathologist (SLP) once a week, both in and out of the classroom. Kelly is not able to speak clearly. Her articulation is severe. She has some cognitive delay, but her receptive language is almost grade level. Kelly has attended ABC school since kindergarten, and all the teachers know her.

Cindy, her teacher, is glad to have her in the class, as she is a sweet girl, with minimal behavioral issues. She has always had articulation issues, but through the grades, the teachers have modified, accommodated, and/or compensated for Kelly, as have her peers who have attended school with her.

Her teacher's concern is that as she gets older, and moves to middle school, and then high school, the teachers will not be so accommodating and she will struggle to express herself. Cindy has seen moments where Kelly has gotten frustrated in certain situations, both academically and socially, that require more communication and expressive language. Cindy is concerned this could get worse. She decides to speak with the SLP to see if there is anything that can be done to help Kelly as she moves forward in school.

Cindy: I wanted to talk with you about Kelly. I am becoming concerned with her ability to talk. I know she has articulation issues, but she is becoming more and more frustrated in what she wants to say. She wants to talk to the other girls on the playground as well as participate in class discussion, but she can't say what she wants to say. What can we do?

SLP: I have been having the same concerns myself. In fact, I talked with her mother yesterday, and they are seeing her behavior change at home because of not being able to talk with her sister all the time. I have been trying to come up with different strategies.

Cindy: Well, I think it is time we address the issue that she is not going to improve her speech. She is almost 12 years old, what more can be done?

SLP: Not much else. She is a smart girl, and she wants to tell us things, but she can't.

Cindy: OK, then let's come up with another plan.

SLP: I was at a district professional learning community meeting, and this issue came up regarding others students in the district. One idea is that we provide Kelly with a communication device that has a program that allows her to choose pictures that can speak for her. We can program it with whatever picture/words we want. It is totally customizable.

Cindy: Really, how big is this device?

SLP: It does not have to be very big. It is something that can be placed on a phone. She can carry it around and can talk with her friends and in class discussions.

Cindy: That would be great. Do you have a device ready?

SLP: I will have to get one from the district, but I can have one here by tomorrow. I will bring it by the class. I will need to work with her to teach her how to find the pictures at first, but once she gets the hang of it, I think she will be fine.

Cindy: Thank you so much, I think this could really solve a lot of her issues.

SUMMARY

Assistive technology is a tool that allows a student to access the curriculum. It is not a teaching technique and not every student will benefit from the same device. As each student is different, so should be his or her technology. For students with communication difficulties, an augmentative communication device will become their voice. For a student with fine motor issues, a speech-to-text app will be their writing tool. Assistive technology will allow students to be "equal" to their peers.

BIBLIOGRAPHY

Friend, Marilyn, & Bursuck, William D. (2009). *Including students with special needs: A practical guide for classroom teachers* (5th ed.). Upper Saddle River, NJ: Pearson.

Inglis, A. D. (2010/2011, December/January). *Smart inclusion for the 21st century classroom*. Retrieved from www.closingthegap.com.

Shrieber, O. E. (2004). Word processing as an assistive technology tool for enhancing academic outcomes for students with writing disabilities in a general education classrooom. *Journal of Learning Disabilities, 37*(2), 143–154.

Templeton, H. L. (2008). Ensuring equal access to technology: Providing assistive technology to students with disabilities. *Theory into Practice, 47*, 212–219. doi: 10.1080/00405840802153874.

Wehmeyer, Michael L., Sean J. Smith, Susan B. Palmer, Daniel K. Davies (2004). Technology use by students with intellectual disabilities: An overview. *Journal of Special Education Technology, 19*, pp. 7–21.

Wilson, Carolyn H., Wilson, Carolyn H., Brice, Costeena, Carter, Emanuel I., Fleming, Jeffery C., Hay, Dontia D., Hicks, John D., Picot, Ebony, Taylor, Aashja M., & Weaver, Jessica (2011). *Familiar technology promotes academic success for students with exceptional learning needs.*

Chapter 8

What are Professional Learning Communities?

Never doubt that a small group of committed, thoughtful people can change the world: Indeed it's the only thing that ever has!

Margaret Mead

Professional learning communities (PLCs) are meetings organized around groups of teachers teaching the same grade level, grade span, or content area. In a PLC, teachers come together regularly to review student data, discuss appropriate intervention, and develop lessons that provide high-quality first lessons that move the students forward in their learning. PLCs are a formalized collaboration among teachers who work in a defined way to determine which lessons for which students will produce academic learning results by questioning each other, promoting deep thinking, and developing effective instruction.

Rick DuFour (2004), the leader in promoting PLCs, says, "The professional learning community model flows from the assumption that the core mission of formal education is not simply to ensure that students are taught but to ensure that they learn. This simple shift—from a focus on teaching to a focus on learning—has profound implications for schools." Those implications include teacher participation, time devoted to PLCs, and a cultural shift "*from teaching to learning.*" Let's look at these more in depth.

TEACHER PARTICIPATION

For PLCs to work, teachers must be willing to meet and share with their colleagues. We know that staff lounges and classrooms where teachers congregate after school are a beehive of conversation and collaborations, but are these discussions focused on student learning? Teachers want and need to talk to one another. They do it whenever they are not in front of a classroom of students. However, the collaboration of the PLC type needs teachers who want to discuss how to be better teachers and more knowledgeable about student progress.

Interestingly, research on millennials, those born between 1980 and 2000, shows that they not only want to collaborate, but it is a necessity for this group which has the largest number of people in the workforce at this time (Lewis, 2014). So, if collaboration were felt as a necessity, one would think that setting up PLCs in schools and districts would be easy.

Unfortunately, over a decade after the introduction of PLCs, districts are finding it difficult to implement. The reasons are plenty, but mostly revolve around issues related to work requirements and time. Teachers need to find the time and see the value of this type of collaboration. That's where administrators and teacher leaders come into the equation. Their role will be discussed in Chapter 10 on leadership support, but for now let's take a look at the issue of time.

DESIGNATED TIME

PLCs are *regularly scheduled time* for teachers to really delve deep into what their students are learning. If teachers on a grade level or content area assign the same task, they can review all of the students' work from multiple classrooms or samples from each room. Arranging for this dedicated time takes planning. It takes developing a schedule that allows teachers distraction-free time to discuss student learning. Some examples of how schools manage to find time for PLCs follow:

1. Some districts have instituted a 4 + 1 schedule that allows for four longer instructional days and one shorter instructional day that include time for the PLC. The PLC can be held before students arrive or after they leave.

2. Other districts provide a stipend for the additional time that is scheduled for PLCs.

3. Another option is to bring in multiple substitute teachers one day a month so the teachers can rotate through a grade level or department every hour-and-a-half.

All three of these models provide opportunities for teachers to be free from all other responsibilities while discussing student learning. Often the site administrator will ask for a written summary of the meeting in order to stay current on teachers' concerns and student learning issues and their progress.

These summaries also allow teachers to reflect over the year how the students have become more proficient. But time must be carved out of busy days and weeks in order for PLCs to work.

CULTURAL SHIFT

PLCs are *a cultural shift from isolation in the classroom to active collaboration with peers.* The shift is constructed on trust and openness. A PLC, to be effective, must be built on trust, trust that "it's OK to divulge my failures and trust that the other members will be by my side and offer assistance."

Trust is a necessity that is sometimes developed over meeting regularly with the same group of teachers. If trust is evident, it will allow teachers to be open and be able to analyze what the students have learned, what concepts need additional instruction, and where intervention is needed with confidence. This openness in discussing student work and progress is a valuable exercise for any teacher, but for a teacher of students with disabilities, it allows for understanding what grade-level work looks like and how instruction needs to be altered for certain students.

For all teachers in a PLC, the review of student work provides a way to develop rubrics for future evaluations, allows for the identification of students needing extra help, and assists the teachers in determining what instructional strategies and formative assessments should be used in the future. A PLC is a cultural shift to trust in one's peers and an openness to share both the positive and the negative in teaching and student learning.

MEETING THE NEEDS OF ALL STUDENTS

Working in a PLC allows teachers of general and special education to work together to make adaptations, accommodations, and exemptions for students with disabilities so they may continue to access rigorous state standards. Additionally, special education teachers have specific skills in scaffolding instruction for greater understanding by the students. In a PLC, these teachers can share their various strengths with the outcome being a better instructional experience for all students.

CONTENT OF A PLC

PLCs are not grade-level meetings and should not be used for scheduling, or other routine tasks. PLCs are about *teaching and learning.* Teachers in a PLC need to be asking some of the following questions of themselves and each other during the meeting:

1. How can I change my teaching in order to reach all of my students, including students with disabilities, with first-time instruction?

2. How can I plan my lessons and units in advance using research-based practices like UDL and formative assessment?

3. How can I construct tasks that are interesting to the students, but hone in on the specific standards I am teaching? Can I include more differentiated instruction?

4. What formative assessment strategies need to be embedded into my lessons to assure all students are moving their learning forward?

5. How will I know my students have learned the lesson being taught? What will I do if they haven't?

6. Did this assignment/task/assessment give me enough information to know what students know? How do I know? What was missing?

7. How can I differentiate my teaching to reach all of the learning groups in my class? Are my students with disabilities progressing?

8. Is my pacing too fast? Too slow? Just right? How do I know?

9. What strategies are my colleagues using that result in success for their students? For their students with disabilities? Can I implement those strategies? What might be the result?

10. Are all of my students learning and mastering concepts?

There are many more questions that teachers can ask themselves and each other in a PLC. The more questions generated, the richer the discussion about individual teacher's instruction, student learning, and student misconceptions. What questions would you ask in a PLC?

SCENARIO

At the end of a shortened teaching day, 6th-grade teachers begin their PLC meeting.

Kalyn: As this week's facilitator of our PLC, I'd like to go over our agenda for the day. As we agreed upon last month, we would all teach the Greek history unit and give the same performance and written test at the end of the unit. So with that in mind, here is our agenda for today's meeting:

1. Discuss the positive outcomes of teaching the unit for you as a teacher and your students. (10 minutes)

2. Discuss changes that will need to be made for next year's lesson. (10 minutes)

3. Determine if the performance task was appropriate to determine what our students had learned. (20 minutes)

4. Analyze the written test for student understanding, retesting needs, or reviewing concepts. (25 minutes)

5. Next agenda. (10 minutes)

We only have an hour and 15 minutes, so we need to be efficient but thorough in our discussions. Nancy, you're our timekeeper, so will you quickly review our norms to keep us on task and on time?

Nancy: Our norms are simple:

*   Start and end on time
*   Stay on topic of student learning
*   Listen to each other
*   Let everyone have a chance to talk
*   Silence cell phones
*   Ask questions

Kalyn:	Thank you, Nancy. If everyone agrees with the norms, let's start the meeting. (All agree to the norms.) Our first item is "Discuss the positive outcomes of teaching the unit for you as a teacher and your students." We have 10 minutes on this item. Mark, will you take notes as our record keeper? Who would like to begin?
Linda:	I found the students very engaged in the idea of democracy. I think having the primary elections being a current topic allowed the students to really have practical events they could relate to and transfer that knowledge to ancient times.
Ron:	I started the unit with a discussion around the current election cycle. I found that my students were also more involved in the present situation, and at times it was quite a lively discussion as they all began to take sides of the current candidates. I think I was surprised by how much they knew and were passionate about in current politics! It was then easy to translate that into the ancient Greek forums.

Mark:	Another huge positive was the acting out of the forums. This really helped my students with disabilities as they processed the content of the unit. They were intrigued that the Greeks invented theater, as we know it today. The plays and student acting were really a positive way to reach students about concepts so ancient.
Nancy:	I think building all the acting into this unit was a positive as well, but what really captured my students' imagination and excitement was re-enacting the Olympics. It is especially relevant with the Olympics being held this year. The students thought it was brilliant that the Olympics were started to honor the Greek's gods. And of course, looking up and studying about each of the gods brought on a lot of laughter, but they learned all about them quite quickly! The concept of multiple gods was quite new to many of them. It was great to see my more physically challenged students compete in teams and share the success, which is usually fleeting for them.
Kalyn:	So far we have as positives the current election, which allowed students to relate to ancient times, acting out many of the forums and theater productions of the Greeks and staging the Olympics after researching the various gods of the Greeks. I agree with all three of these as ways that engaged my students in the unit. The readings became more intriguing to them as they wanted to find out more about these ancient people that laid the framework for our current society. Let's move to our next agenda item "Discuss changes that will need to be made for next year's lesson."
Mark:	Well, we won't have a major election next year, so we really need to think about how we engage the students in democracy. Maybe we should plan to teach this unit around student body elections.
Ron:	That's a great idea. Also, the city council has its elections in an off year from national elections, so we could invite the candidates to our school to discuss the process with our students. That would be a great introduction into this unit and would help struggling students and students with disabilities with some pre-lesson material.
Nancy:	I know we are talking about what needs to be changed, but I think we should hold on this item until we review the student data on the performance task and the unit test.
Kalyn:	We have a suggestion to hold this item, do you agree? (All agree to move to the third agenda item.) Alright, let's look at item #3, "Determine if the performance task was appropriate to determine what our students had learned."
Linda:	Well, I think the students did a great job with our performance task: "Students are to use the information and research from our unit to become museum archivists. The task is to gather photos, create

images and artifacts, and share facts and stories. These artifacts will be displayed in a museum. Each piece on exhibit must have a detailed explanation of what it is and why it was chosen. The goal of the museum is to portray the lasting cultural and political events of ancient Greece that contribute to our society today."

As we agreed, I randomly put my students into four groups. Each group was responsible for art, politics, theater, and Olympics. I gave each group the rubric we developed together to determine their grade. Two of my groups scored a 4, the highest score possible and the other two groups scored a 3. I had the groups score each other's projects as well and the results were the same. I was impressed that they were so critical in their viewing of the projects. I was impressed at how much they had learned during the course of the unit.

Mark: I basically did the same thing. Since I have a cluster of gifted students as well as students with disabilities, I chose not to do random groups. I carefully, selected each of the groups, making sure that the gifted and students with disabilities were distributed evenly. By giving the students the rubric in advance, they were really able to define their own score. I had one group with a 4, two groups with a 3, and one group with a 2. I have given that group with the score of 2, time to revise their project and turn it in to me by next week. I know this was supposed to be a final project, but I felt that student learning was more important than the date that the task was finished. I hope you all don't mind that I made this modification. My key gate student in that group was out with an operation, and I didn't feel like her group should be punished by her absence. (All agree it was a good idea to give them more time.)

Ron: I split my students into four groups as well, but they all had to research all four contents of art, politics, theater, and Olympics. I just felt they all needed to own the information. It was more complex grading them. No group received a 4 in any area, and I have to admit that a 2 was the most prominent score in my class.

Nancy: Ron why do you think your scores were so much lower than Linda's or Mark's?

Ron: I've been trying to figure that out. I don't think they understood the concepts as well as the students in Linda or Mark's class.

Linda: Do you think it might have something to do with how you assigned the concepts?

Ron: Hmm, I hadn't thought of that as I figured it would be better for them to know in depth about all of the concepts. But now listening to the rest of you, I think I miscalculated. If I had divided up the tasks as the rest of you did, maybe each student would have been more knowledgeable in at least one area. I have to think about this a little more. You know I'm new to this group work stuff and I really want to know how each student is doing. But you all had success with your groups, so I trust that it works. Thanks for sharing.

Kalyn: That's a good segue into our fourth agenda item, "Analyze the written test for student understanding, retesting needs, or reviewing concepts." Let's see how the students did when they had to answer questions independently.

Linda: The day before I gave the test, we reviewed everything in our "museum." I had the students do an exit card on the exhibit that gave them the most new information. Well, of course, they had to read everything! The next day I gave the test. I'm glad we asked higher-order questions because I got some great answers. The multiple-choice questions were adjusted to the struggling students and were more factual in nature. So, the question that stymied the entire class was "How and why has the Parthenon been used through the ages?" The answers were light compared to the question about Athena which all got right in both the short-answer and multiple-choice questions. I think I need to revisit this concept.

Mark: Mine had difficulty as well. I think we need to review how the Parthenon is presented in the text to see if it aligns with what questions we were asking. Hey, that's something to put on our list for item 2 on the agenda!

Ron: It was hard on my students as well. They seemed to do OK on all the other questions, but really bombed that one.

Nancy: I will join the chorus. I think *we* need to review the text and other information we provided.

Kalyn: Alright, I think we have a pretty solid trend that the students grasped everything but the information on the Parthenon. My students also did poorly on that short-answer question. Let's analyze how we asked the question and what we taught that would help the students.

The meeting goes on with all of the participants joining in on the discussions.

STRATEGIES FOR PROFESSIONAL LEARNING COMMUNITIES

The scenario offers many hints for making a PLC successful. Let's review them in detail.

1. *Facilitator*: This is a key leadership role that can be constant or rotating, as the group prefers. It is a vital position for a successful PLC as the facilitator keeps the group on task and directs leading questions to the group to stay focused on student learning.

2. *Timekeeper*: The person in this role keeps everyone within the time-frames agreed upon by the group. Since most PLCs are between one and two hours, it is important to stick to the times allocated. As in our scenario earlier, the important information was gleaned from the last couple of questions, but the first questions were important to set the stage. If time ran out before getting to question 4, the teachers would not have determined a key flaw in the unit and assessments.

3. *Record keeper*: As mentioned earlier in the chapter, many administrators want a summary of what takes place. Having someone other than the facilitator (who is already busy) and the timekeeper who has an eye on the clock allows for a free flow of information that is captured for all to review at a later date. A year from now when the teachers in our scenario begin the unit on ancient Greece, they will have valuable information to refer to in designing changes for the unit.

4. *Agenda with times allocated*: The practice of having a set agenda with a time allocation gives everyone an idea of the scope and importance of the item. In our scenario, it was questions 3 and 4 that had the most time allocated, because they were the most important questions on the agenda. Teachers knew that a lively discussion would be held on these items.

5. *Norms*: Every group should have agreed-upon norms. They can be few in number (preferred) or up to 8 or 10 in number. Having them and referring to them at every meeting keeps the focus on the meeting and what has to be accomplished. Everyone knows what behavior is expected.

6. *Discussion*: The facilitator's job is to keep the discussion going through-out the meeting. Everyone should join in and give data and impressions of the item in question. If it is a small group, the facilitator can go around in a circle, giving each person a chance to reply. Or the facilitator could use a formative assessment (see Chapter 5) strategy to call on people randomly or make sure everyone has a chance to speak.

7. *Questions*: The more questions that are asked, the deeper the participants will get in the discussion, solution, or next steps. Encourage them of each other, and probe deeply.

8. *Support*: Our last chapter is about leadership support, but support here is for each other. Going into a PLC knowing you will receive help and be able to offer it will allow for a positive use of your time and valuable time

spent moving your students forward. Be supportive of each other as you learn together!

SUMMARY

The concept of a PLC is collaboration. Together we are more than we are individually, so talking together about student progress and learning is one of the keys to student success.

> To deal with the impact of globalization and rapid change, new ways of approaching learning seem to be required. Learning can no longer be left to individuals. To be successful in a changing and increasingly complex world, it is suggested that whole school communities need to work and learn together to take charge of change, finding the best ways to enhance young people's learning. (Stoll, Bolam et al., 2006)

Through the literature on PLCs words, such supportive process, collaboration, a culture of trust and shared values, shared leadership, and learning and teaching are key. So what is your plan for implementing PLCs? We know that when we work together, we have better results for our students, deeper knowledge, and understanding for the teachers and a solid culture of trust and collaboration through a cycle of continuous inquiry, analysis, and action. PLCs will help promote improved learning for all of our students!

BIBLIOGRAPHY

DuFour, R. (2004, May). What is a professional learning community? *Educational Leadership, 8*(61), 6–11.

DuFour, R., Esker, R., & Karhanek, G. (2004). *Whatever it takes: How Professional learning communities respond when kids don't learn.* Solution Tree, Bloomington, Indiana.

Lewis, M. (2014). *Survey: What do 16–21 year-olds say about the language of business.* Retrieved from https://www.virgin.com/virgin-unit/leadership-and-advocacy/survey-what-do-16–21-year-olds-say -about-the-language-of-business.

Stoll, R. L. (2006). Leadership communities: A review of the literature. *Journal of Educational Change, 7,* 221–258. doi: 10.1007/s10833–006–0001–8.

Chapter 9

What Is Co-Teaching?

The most valuable resource that every teacher has is each other. Without collaboration our growth is limited to our own perspectives.

Robert John Meehan

Co-teaching, or cooperative teaching, has become an instructional method implemented to provide access to the general education curriculum for students with disabilities. Co-teaching is commonly known as two teachers, usually a general and special education teacher, working together in the same classroom to provide instruction to all levels of students.

As an inclusionary practice, co-teaching has multiple benefits for students with and without disabilities. Co-teaching allows the general education teacher and the special education teacher to work together to create lessons and present instruction that can meet the needs of all students in the classroom. Co-teaching is also a way for students with disabilities to gain access to the curriculum through inclusive practices in the general education classroom.

With two teachers, there is more opportunity to address these requirements. Co-teaching also allows for teachers to engage in small group or individualized instruction, to modify lessons to address academic needs and allow all students to engage in a common task regardless of learning issues. Co-teaching not only addresses the academic needs of students with disabilities but the social aspects as well. Interaction with peers in a classroom allows both students with and without disabilities to interact and engage in activities that foster positive communication skills, increased empathy, and acceptance of people who are different from each other.

The benefits of co-teaching not only impact the students but the teachers as well. Taking time to plan and collaborate on lessons and develop instructional levels that meet the needs of the students is an aspect of teaching that rarely gets addressed. Too many teachers teach in isolation, and co-teaching allows for discussion and sharing of ideas on how to teach students in a variety of ways. Granted, each teacher brings his or her own strengths and weaknesses to teaching, but good team teaching allows for each teacher to utilize his or her strengths in the most effective way.

For the scope of this chapter, there are six types of models that can be implemented as effective for collaboration. These models should be implemented depending on the strengths of the teachers, the needs of the students, and the structure of the classroom. Not every model will work for all teachers, nor will only one model work all the time. Adapting and adjusting the models will take planning and communication.

MODELS OF COOPERATIVE TEACHING

1. *One teaches, one observes:* One teacher instructs whole group, while the other teacher observes students, possibly collecting data in an academic, behavioral, or social context and taking notes on specific students or the class group to share with the co-teacher after.

2. *Station teaching:* Instruction is divided into three parts. Students are divided into three groups and rotate from station to station. Teachers instruct at two stations, and the students are expected to work independently at the third station.

3. *Parallel teaching:* The class is divided into two equal parts. Each teacher instructs the same material with the intent of being able to differentiate instruction to a smaller group of students and encourage greater student participation.

4. *Alternative teaching:* The class is divided into two groups, one large group and one small group. One teacher instructs the larger group, while the other works with the smaller group for remediation, enrichment, assessment, pre-teaching, or any other purpose seemed necessary for this group. The groups are not fixed and can be rearranged at any time.

5. *Team teaching:* Both teachers instruct the whole class in the same content, with each teacher emphasizing their specific strengths and possibly integrating subjects to meet the needs of all the students.

6. *One teaches, one assists:* One teacher instructs the whole class, while the other teacher circulates around the class, offering individual assistance to specific students.

SCENARIO 1

Lisa M. and Jack K. are teachers at ABC elementary school. Lisa M. has a 4th-grade, general education classroom, and Jack K. teaches special education. Their principal, Ms. North, has asked them to co-teach this year. The school is moving to a full inclusion model, and although the staff agreed to the move, co-teaching is new to most of the teachers. Co-teaching requires planning and the ability to work with others in a close environment. It also requires Lisa and Jack to work together to teach the wide range of students in the class. When developing a co-teaching classroom, many issues must be discussed.

- What type of co-teaching will be best, and which type is each teacher comfortable with?
- How best to resolve conflicts or disagreements?
- What roles will each teacher have, and who will be responsible for what?

Even though Jack has come into Lisa's class to present a lesson or two each month, they have never co-taught a lesson, let alone a whole classroom. Lisa and Jack agree to meet before the school year to discuss these issues.

Lisa:	Jack, thank you so much for meeting today. I am very excited about the new school year although, I will admit, I am a little nervous about us working together. I have not done co-teaching before and to share my classroom will be different.
Jack:	Lisa, I agree with you. I have never co-taught either. I am anxious about how we will work together.
Lisa:	What are your thoughts on an inclusive classroom? Do you think this can work?
Jack:	Well, knowing the students who will be in the classroom, I think we can make this work if we have the right program in place.
Lisa:	Yeah, I agree. How should we decide to plan this year?
Jack:	We should probably first discuss what each of us will be responsible for within the classroom. Like, how are we going to develop the lessons?
Jack:	Well, what kind of co-teaching do you think would work well for us?
Lisa:	At the professional development day they mentioned the different types of co-teaching. It may be something we work out as we go along.

Jack:	True.
Lisa:	I know there are subjects that I feel really comfortable teaching, and I am sure you have some that you like teaching.
Jack:	Yes. Besides my special education background, I do enjoy teaching some core curriculum.
Lisa:	We will have to set some time aside for planning each week. How should we do this? Are you willing to meet 15–20 minutes before or after school twice a week to plan and discuss what is and is not working? Also, we will have to include Betty, the paraprofessional, so she knows what is happening in the class.
Jack:	What about adaptive PE, occupational therapy, and speech and language? They need to be included in the planning as well.
Lisa:	That's right. We will need more time than that. During the day may be the only time to meet with everybody. Maybe Ms. North could have one of the school aides come to the class once a week and read to the students while we meet? Or, what if we joined forces with Gayle and Cliff? They are co-teaching 5th grade and will also need planning time.
Jack:	That's right, too. How about we offer to take each other's class once a week for 30 minutes so we can meet with our team and plan?
Lisa:	Yes, that is a good idea. Let's talk to Ms. North and see what she thinks. And as for our co-teaching model, let's try different methods until we find the one that works for us.

SCENARIO 2

Gayle and Cliff are 6th-grade teachers at XYZ Middle School. Cliff teaches history, and Gayle teaches English. They will be co-teaching a block curriculum class and are discussing the best approach.

Cliff:	So Gayle, are you ready for the new year?
Gayle:	Yes, I think so. We need to discuss how we will approach this new block curriculum. I think we can really integrate the content, but how do you want to approach the teaching part? I am not sure what I feel comfortable with.
Cliff:	I am not sure either. Have you seen our student list for the year? We have quite a few students who have IEPs and 504s. Many have some form of processing issues.

Gayle: Yes, and Cindy, the special education SDC teacher, wants to talk with us about including some of the higher functioning students into our block. She thinks they would benefit from the instruction. She will send an aide with them.

Cliff: Well, OK then. We have to do some planning. What approach are we going to use?

Gayle: I was thinking that we may want to incorporate a few different ones depending on the type of lesson. For example, to introduce a lesson, what if we did a team teaching model? We can teach the whole group, together. We can introduce those parts of the lesson that we each have a strength in. That way the students know we are equal in the class.

Cliff: Good idea. Since we will be integrating history and English, we can each present our subject.

Gayle: Yes, then as we get into the specifics of the content, maybe we can divide the class into two halves, teach the content and, where necessary, differentiate the instruction for those students who need it.

Cliff: Yes, alternative teaching. I have done that before. It can work very well when a group of students are struggling with a concept. We could even switch if we teach our subject strength on different days.

Gayle: Yes. Good idea.

Cliff: OK, then as we get into very specific assignments, we could try station teaching once in a while. Having the students working on independent assignments while we coach them through concepts in groups would be great.

Gayle: Yes, that will work well with students with IEPs and 504s. Really, more individualized instruction is what we need to achieve.

Cliff: On some days, I assume the class will be more content-heavy in one subject than in the other. Are you comfortable in observing or assisting while I teach the class?

Gayle: I am if you are. HA-HA. Yes, I think as we learn more about each other and our teaching styles, we will be able to incorporate many models that will work for our students. We will just have to see which ones the students respond to the best and go from there.

Cliff: I agree. I look forward to our partnership this year.

Gayle: So do I.

STRATEGIES FOR CO-TEACHING

Not every co-teaching model will work for all teachers, but being able to identify which type works best for you and your students will allow for flexible teaching, meeting student needs and providing access to curriculum for all students effectively. (See figure 9.1.)

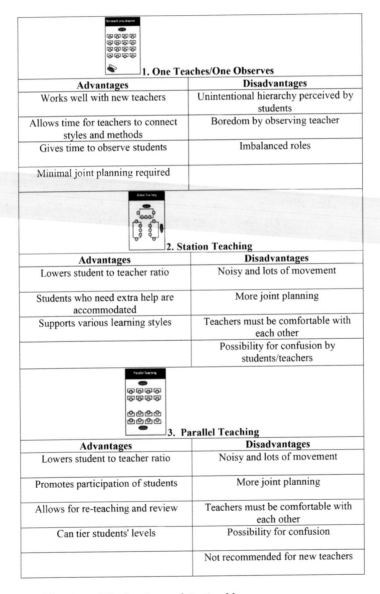

1. One Teaches/One Observes

Advantages	Disadvantages
Works well with new teachers	Unintentional hierarchy perceived by students
Allows time for teachers to connect styles and methods	Boredom by observing teacher
Gives time to observe students	Imbalanced roles
Minimal joint planning required	

2. Station Teaching

Advantages	Disadvantages
Lowers student to teacher ratio	Noisy and lots of movement
Students who need extra help are accommodated	More joint planning
Supports various learning styles	Teachers must be comfortable with each other
	Possibility for confusion by students/teachers

3. Parallel Teaching

Advantages	Disadvantages
Lowers student to teacher ratio	Noisy and lots of movement
Promotes participation of students	More joint planning
Allows for re-teaching and review	Teachers must be comfortable with each other
Can tier students' levels	Possibility for confusion
	Not recommended for new teachers

Figure 9.1   Advantages/Disadvantages of Co-Teaching
Source: Daniel Moonasar, 2014, with permission.

4. Alternate Teaching

Advantages	Disadvantages
Lowers student to teacher ratio	Noisy and lots of movement
Students who need extra help are accommodated	Can stigmatize smaller groups
Can tier students' levels	More joint planning
Allows for re-teaching and review	Possibility of confusion

5. Team Teaching

Advantages	Disadvantages
Allows for creativity in lesson delivery	Requires a lot of joint planning time/commitment
Works extremely well for teachers who are familiar with each other	Most difficult to implement
Accommodates for hybrid methods of co-teaching	Dependent on teaching styles and methods
	Not recommended for new teachers

6. One Teaches/One Assists

Advantages	Disadvantages
Works well with new teachers	Unintentional hierarchy perceived by students
Allows time for teachers to connect styles and methods	Assisting teacher can be a distraction
Allows students to receive extra help	Students can become dependent on the assisting teacher
Improved classroom management	Imbalances roles of teachers

Figure 9.1 (Continued)

The charts identify significant advantages and disadvantages for each co-teaching model. Not every model will work all the time. Depending on the needs of the students and the makeup of the classroom, a different model will work one day, and then another will work the next. Also, depending on the strengths of the teachers, one model may be more effective than the other. Experiment with different models to see which works best for you.

SUMMARY

For co-teaching to be beneficial for students, many issues must be addressed for it to be successful. Important components include both general and special education teachers' attitude, sufficient planning time, voluntary participation, mutual respect, administrative support, staff development opportunities, and a shared philosophy of instruction and behavior management. Not every classroom can have co-teaching all day, but a lesson or two once a day or once a week will benefit all students.

BIBLIOGRAPHY

Friend, M., Cook, L., Hurley-Chamberlain, D., & Shamberger, C. (2010). Co-teaching: An illustration of the complexity of collaboration in special education. *Journal of Educational and Psychological Consultation, 20*, 9–27. doi: 10.1080/10474410903535380.

Hunt, P., Soto, G., Maier, J., & Doering, K. (2003). Collaborative teaming to support students at risk and students with severe disabilities in general education classroom. *Exceptional Children, 69*(3), 315–332.

Marcus, T. H. (2007). Closing the achievement gap through teacher collaboration: Facilitating multiple trajectories for teacher learning. *Journal of Advanced Academics, 19*(1), 116–138.

Moonasar, Daniel. (2014, December 24). How to make it work: Co-teaching in South Korea. *EPIK UCC Daegu Training.* Retrieved from http://pt.slideshare.net/LienadRasanoom/models-of-coteaching-part-a.

Scruggs, Thomas E., Margo, A., Mastropieri, & Kimberly A. Mcduffie. (2007). Co-teaching in an inclusive classroom: A metasynthesis of qualitative research. *Council for Exceptional Children, 73*(4), 392–416.

Chapter 10

What Is Leadership Support?

If your actions inspire others to dream more, learn more, do more and become more, you are a leader.

John Quincy Adams

If you are a teacher reading this book, you are probably saying to yourself, "Well, this is all great information, but I can't decide independently what kinds of grouping strategies the school will use, or assume other teachers will agree to use UDL or formative assessment strategies. So what should I do?"

This chapter will assist teachers, principals, and district office staff in the implementation of the strategies presented in this book. To do so it will be important to look at all levels of support by administrators, including central office and individual department's personnel, principals, assistant principals, and other administrators. And let's not forget the support from fellow teachers.

NEW VISION, NEW ROLES

For District and School Leaders

District and school leaders actually hold the key to the successful implementation of programs to meet today's rigorous standards for all students and especially students with disabilities. These leaders must be willing to set a vision around the concept that all students can learn. All teachers are responsible to all students to make the learning environment engaging for maximum mastery.

Many districts have implemented professional learning communities (PLCs) to promote the vision for teachers to interact and take responsibility for meeting the needs of all students. By supporting PLCs, these leaders provide a forum for teachers, not only to work together closely, but to develop trusting relationships that would allow for co-teaching, active engagement around all students' learning, and the strengthening of the instructional strategies presented in this book. PLCs are powerful tools to promote student learning as teachers focus on data-driven results and the impact of selected instructional strategies on student learning.

In order to carry out this vision, district and site leadership must be willing to reallocate funds that allow for teacher interaction. These funds may be used for additional personnel, professional development programs that support the research-based strategies in this book, and time for "teacher talk." It will only be through the collaboration of general and special education teachers that progress will be made for all students.

For Special Education Teachers

The new role for teachers of students with disabilities is to envision being a leader in the collaboration between and among general education teachers. This is a critical role change for special education teachers—to take the lead! Develop partnerships with general education teachers by assisting them with strategies to implement in their classrooms or help with student issues that may arise when the general education teacher is frustrated. This will show your leadership and care for all students.

When strong bonds of trust are built, better program and instruction will be developed and implemented for all students. With strong bonds forged, teachers will be more willing to be co-teachers in the academic advancement of both general and special education students. They will be willing to add their curriculum and instructional strengths to the delivery of a rigorous curriculum. With this type of partnership teachers of both general education and special education will be able to provide individual support for all learners—struggling and achieving!

The teachers of students with disabilities have special skills that help support individual students behaviorally, as well as academically. They can provide their expertise in data analysis, task analysis, and behavioral analysis. Additionally, the skills of the general education teacher in the areas of curriculum development and instructional strategies will support students throughout the learning process. What a difference a team makes!!

For General Education Teachers

A new role and vision for general education teachers is one of sharing and advocacy for the students with disabilities in their care. As content experts, they can lead the discussion within their schools around the content standards and curriculum needs. Their data-driven instruction and teaching can assist their counterparts on utilizing screening data from formative and summative assessments. It can assist in developing differentiated instruction and conducting student progress monitoring for all students.

Additionally, after analyzing data, teachers will be able to make meaningful instructional decisions based on the ongoing progress monitoring of all students. Working in professional learning communities the general education teachers share data and student progress with all the teachers in the PLC and use each other as resources for making adjustments throughout the instructional day.

SCENARIO

It is the last faculty meeting of the school year, and the principal, Mr. Watts, begins to set the stage for the next school year.

Mr. Watts: I am so proud of all of you and what we have been able to accomplish this year as a team. I thought as we wrap up the year, it would be a good time to begin a discussion for next year while our successes and needs are fresh in our mind. I'd like to begin by talking about our program for students with disabilities. This year, we focused on team teaching during English-language arts. How do you feel that went?

Andrew: I was surprised at how well it went. Megan and I were able to use each other's strengths as we worked with the general education students and the students with disabilities.

Megan: Yes, I agree. As the teacher of students with disabilities, I wasn't sure how the students would accept me or how Andrew and I were going to coordinate the two of us teaching at the same time. Our students all gained from having two experts in the room.

Shannon: I didn't team teach this year with a special education teacher, but we worked in our PLC together. It was amazing how much I understand data with Maggie's help! With her background in special education she was able to help me understand more in depth the data I was collecting on students.

Teachers continue to share how the limited team teaching worked in their classrooms.

Mr. Watts: So, it appears that what we did this year really worked! I'd like to think about moving as many students with disabilities into full inclusion next year and moving our team teaching to a co-teaching model. I read a book called *What's Missing* recently, and I think with the trust and bonds you have all built through the PLC process we could learn together and provide a rigorous, but appropriate setting for all of our students. How many of you know about the full inclusion model? (Hands are raised by a few teachers.) I thought it would be a good idea if we read the chapter on placement strategies together today.

Mr. Watts hands out the chapter. After reading silently, he asks teachers to pair up to talk about what they read. He asks Jeff to chart the responses of each group as they report out.

Mr. Watts: It appears that we have come up with a few generalized comments from the chapter.

1. Full Inclusion should be a viable, least restrictive environment for students.

2. Students with disabilities gain from interacting with academically stronger students.

3. Full Inclusion isn't for every student or for every teacher.

4. Teachers of general and special education must work in close collaboration to make full inclusion effective.

5. Teachers of general and special education must have a strong trusting bond to work together.

Shannon: I think after reading this chapter I need additional professional development to really make this successful.

Megan: I agree. Is there someone we can bring in either from the district or a consultant to help us understand all of the issues and steps we would need to take? Also, there is a reference to formative assessment as really helping students achieve. I think we need some help in that area as well.

Mr. Watts: Well, the district office supports us in our efforts. The offices of special education and curriculum and instruction have both set aside funding for schools to use for summer and fall training on topics of our choice that lead to the least restrictive environment for all students and promote learning. Who would like to be on a planning team that will meet next week to get our plans in motion?

Andrew: I would.

Megan: So would I.

Shannon: I'd like to volunteer as well.

Mr. Watts: I think that will be a good size committee. Please report back to us by email what you decide for our professional development.

STRATEGIES FOR LEADERSHIP SUPPORT

District Office Personnel Supporting Teaching and Learning

1. *Working with principals on improving instruction*
    Principals need coaches, book clubs, and professional development in best practices in teaching and learning. Coaches provide confidential help to principals, helping them understand new strategies and strengthening existing knowledge of strategies they are currently practicing.
    Book clubs give all leadership staff a way to understand and implement instructional strategies, placement strategies, and programs better. As they work through a book together, they learn from each other and from the material being read.
    Professional development in instructional and placement strategies is imperative for all students to succeed with rigorous content standards. Principals in turn need to become experts in order to coach and assist the teachers at the school site.

2. *Supporting the curriculum and instruction leadership director(s)*
    Central office staff also needs to support and have an entrepreneurial spirit to help principals and teachers learn new skills. As they support the sites, the superintendent, including offering training on how to improve their work with principals, too must support them. This can be done with budgets that allow for professional development, in retreats and regular monthly administrative meetings. Central office personnel need to be freed up of as much "adminstrivia" as possible in order to spend time with principals at their sites. Central office administrators often know individual schools well and can help with decision making and problem solving in the area of teaching and learning.

3. *Communicating the vision*
    Leaders in the central office need to communicate well enough so that principals, central office employees, private donors, and other key players

can understand the work, know why it matters, and then lend their support. Communication should be ongoing through websites, newsletters, newspapers, Twitter™, Facebook™, and any other social media platform a district uses. Communicating the vision includes notifying all the stakeholders as to why instructional and placement strategies will be used in the district, as well as the intended results and the actual results. It's time to shine!

4. *Gathering and using information to guide the effort*
   District leadership should support the use of data to drive instruction. The use of data includes the work of PLCs, state testing, benchmark assessments, interim assessments, and demographic data. Use every piece of data you have to guide your district through the implementation of instructional and placement strategies!

Principals Supporting Teaching and Learning

1. *Budget development around the vision*
   Develop a practical budget to implement the desired instructional and placement strategies selected. To develop a budget, it is important to have a clear vision for where the students are going. Be sure to reach consensus with the staff on the direction of the instructional and placement strategies that students will need to meet the rigorous standards expected of them.

2. *Survey your teachers*
   It is important to determine the professional development needs of the staff when implementing new strategies. Plan for individual and group training that will move your staff through the goals they want to attain for their students.

3. *Determine space, equipment, and material needs*
   As the site leader, teachers will be coming to you to fulfill their needs. In order for a successful implementation, teachers will need classroom space to co-teach, or plastic cups to implement traffic lighting techniques, or a variety of leveled books on the same topic to differentiate. It is best to be prepared and to ask teachers what they need and then as a staff prioritize what goes into the budget.

4. *Know what they know*
   Principals should have a general knowledge of research-based instructional and placement strategies the teachers want to implement. This book offers leaders and teachers alike many strategies to choose from. Don't try to implement all of them or you will be overwhelmed!

5. *Teachers need time to work together*

Figure out how to give your teachers collaboration time! Whether you have a formal PLC time that is negotiated or you budget release time on a regular basis, your teachers will need "teacher talk" time. Especially as you are asking teachers of general education and special education to work together, that planning time is essential.

6. *Teachers need you*

Make sure you leave plenty of time in your day for teacher drop in time, classroom observations, and informal conferences. Teachers rely on the expertise of their principal for advice and support. Be that person for them!

GENERAL AND SPECIAL EDUCATION TEACHERS

1. *Professional development needs*

Teachers need and want professional development that is focused on student needs. Ask for it! If you are going to implement differentiated instruction or formative assessment, you need professional development. It could take the form of a conference, a presentation, or an article. Don't be bashful when it comes to meeting the needs of your instruction and your students' progress!

2. *Equipment and material needs*

Think carefully about your plans and what is needed to carry them out. Be strategic when asking for the things you need and make sure that you speak up when it's time to develop the school's budget.

3. *Support for students with disabilities*

Teachers need to be very clear on what support looks like for their students. Does it mean that extra staff is needed? Does it mean that the principal needs to excite the staff toward inclusion? Does it mean that you need time to talk? Any and all of these needs are important, and the list is probably long. Figure out what support you need and voice it!

4. *Support from my principal*

Be proactive with the principal when it comes to needing help with social, emotional, behavioral issues that arise with your students. It would be great to have a discussion with the principal on how you would like help or support.

5. *Feedback*

Ask your principal and fellow teachers to observe you with a new implementation in order to get constructive feedback. When you are not immersed in teaching, you often can catch issues, concerns, or great things happening. Be positive about receiving feedback, and you will see how your teaching improves and your students' progress!

SUMMARY

Leadership support comes from many sources at a school from the principal, other administrators, fellow teachers, and even students. In order for general and special education students to thrive, we must be ready to share leadership with everyone.

BIBLIOGRAPHY

Drolet, B., & Turner, D. (2010). *Building a bridge to success: From program improvement to excellence.* Lanham, MD: Rowman & Littlefield.

Fliegeman, L. (2012). *7 top things teachers want from their principal.* Retrieved from http://www.edutopia.org/stw-school-turnaround-principal-teacher-development-tips.

The General Ed Teacher's Guide to the Inclusive Classroom. (2016). Retrieved from http://www.specialeducationguide.com/pre-k-12/inclusion/the-general-ed-teachers-guide-to-the-inclusive-classroom/education-teacher.

Harvey, T., & Drolet, B. (2004). *Building teams, building people, expanding the fifth resource.* Lanham, MD: Rowman & Littlefield.

Harvey, T. R., Drolet, B. M., & Devore, D. P. (2014). *Leading for excellence: A twelve step program to student achievement.* Lanham, MD: Rowman & Littlefield.

Hirsh, S. (2009, February). The principal's role in supporting learning communities. *Educational Leadership, 66*(5), 22–23.

Survival Guide for New Teachers. (2004). Retrieved from www2.ed.gov: http://www2.ed.gov/teachers/become/about/survivalguide/principal/html.

What Are the Challenges of Being a Special Education Teacher? (2014). Retrieved from://www.special-education-degree.net/what-are-the-challenges-of-being-a-special-ed.

Appendix A

UDL Lesson Template				
Unit/Lesson Topic:		Length of Unit/Lesson	Use Initials Only	
Common Core Standard(s) to be addressed:		Lesson Objective:	Students needing support	enrichment
Target Goal(s):		All:	IEP	
IEP Goal(s):		Most:	504	
UDL Principles to be implemented within lesson:		Some:	BIP	
I. Provide Multiple Means of Representation:		Activity for Lesson	Materials Needed	Day/Date
1. Provide options for perception				
2. Provide options for language, mathematical expressions, and symbols				
3. Provide options for comprehension				
II. Provide Multiple Means for Action and Expression:		Activity for Lesson	Materials Needed	Day/Date
1. Provide options for physical action				
2. Provide options for expression and communication				
3. Provide options for executive functions				
III. Provide Multiple Means for Engagement:		Activity for Lesson	Materials Needed	Day/Date
1. Provide options for recruiting interest				
2. Provide options for sustaining effort and persistence				
3. Provide options for self-regulation				

Appendix B

Key Word Poster

Formative

Techniques

Learning Intentions

Responsibility

Feedback

Success Criteria

Resources

Questioning

5 Key Strategies

Appendix C

SAMPLE RUBRIC

This rubric should be distributed to the class at the beginning of the task.

Assignment:
Name(s):

Category	4	3	2	1	Your score
Main Idea (may be weighted)	The topic and main ideas are clear and easily understood.	Topic is clear and there are some main ideas.	Topic is stated, but main ideas are unclear or ambiguous.	Topic and/or main ideas are absent or very unclear.	
Details (may be weighted)	Interesting details support the main idea.	Some detail is added to support each main idea.	Few details are present to support the main ideas.	Little or no detail is provided for the main ideas.	
Content (may be weighted)	Facts are presented in an engaging and accurate way.	Some accurate facts are included.	Minimal facts are presented.	Facts are not provided.	
Mechanics	Capitalization and punctuation are correct throughout and provide interest to the reader.	Capitalization and punctuation are correct throughout.	There are a few errors in capitalization or punctuation.	There are a many errors in capitalization or punctuation.	
Grammar	There are no grammatical mistakes.	There is at least 1 grammatical mistake.	There are more than two grammatical mistakes.	There are many grammatical mistakes.	
Total					

Appendix D

Sample Rubric Template

Score	Description	Comments
4		
3		
2		
1		

Appendix E

2 Stars and a Wish

★

_____

_____

_____

_____

★

_____

_____

_____

_____

Wish

_____

_____

_____

_____

Appendix F

ABCD Cards

A B

C D

Appendix G

ABCD Cards continued

E F

G T

Appendix H

TRAFFIC LIGHTING - SELF			
Formative Assessment Technique	**Green**	**Yellow**	**Red**
Learning Intentions			
Success Criteria			
Share Exemplars of Student Work			
Key Word Posters			
Rubrics			
Think/Pair/Share			
Carousel			
Partner Learning			
Homework Help Board			
Stand Up, Hand Up, Pair Up			
Jigsaw Learning			
Question Strips with small group			
Stop/Slow Signals			
Question Strips			
Pre-Flight Checklist			
Traffic Lighting Self			
Concept List			

Index

About the Authors

Dr. Carolyn Lindstrom received her bachelor of arts degree from St. Mary's College of California, her master of arts in education administration from Chapman University, and her master of arts in special education from Brandman University where she graduated summa cum laude. She earned her doctorate in organizational leadership from Brandman University.

She has worked in the field of education since 1989. She has taught grades K–12 in general and special education and has been a private school administrator for alternative high schools. She was a founding developer for the first synchronous online high school in the country.

She currently teaches students with moderate to severe disabilities, working with other teachers in collaboration and co-teaching to include all students and providing access to general education curriculum. She has led schoolwide programs and trained teachers in inclusive and instructional practices.

Dr. Lindstrom is an adjunct professor, teaching in both general and special education credentialing departments on collaboration and teaching methods for inclusion. She has worked with state and national organizations developing new teacher credentialing requirements. She has spoken at conferences and presented research on best practices for teaching students with disabilities.

Dr. Carolyn Lindstrom

Dr. Bonita (Bonnie) Drolet received her bachelor of arts and master of arts from California State University, Los Angeles. She received her doctorate in educational management from the University of La Verne.

Her teaching and administrative career includes pre-kindergarten through 8th grade and the university level. After serving as a principal in several districts, she became an assistant superintendent of educational services and led her schools to award-winning status at both the state and federal levels.

She is the coauthor with Thomas Harvey of the book *Building Teams, Building People: Expanding the Fifth Resource* and coauthor with Dr. Deborah Turner of the book *Building a Bridge to Success: From Program Improvement to Excellence*. She coauthored with Dr. Thomas Harvey and Dr. Doug DeVore the book *Leading for Excellence: A Twelve Step Program to Student Achievement*.

She is sought after by many school districts and private enterprises to assist them in building successful organizations. She has consulted with the Department of Education in Washington, DC, city governments, schools, and districts.

She has worked as an educational consultant, working directly with teachers and administrators throughout the nation in team building, organizational leadership, formative assessment, assessing data, and prescribing classroom instruction that will ensure success. Her coaching skills are sought after for new and experienced administrators at all levels.

Dr. Bonita M. Drolet